THE BEST

CATHOLIC

2 0 0 5

WRITING

THE BEST

CATHOLIC

2005

WRITING

EDITED BY

BRIAN DOYLE

LOYOLAPRESS.
CHICAGO

LOYOLAPRESS.

3441 N. ASHLAND AVENUE
CHICAGO, ILLINOIS 60657
(800) 621-1008
WWW.LOYOLABOOKS.ORG

The Bible excerpts in "A Spirituality of Aging" (page 53) and "I Am the Church" (page 197) are taken from the New Revised Standard Version Bible: Catholic Edition, copyright © 1993 and 1989 by the Division of Christian Education of the National Council of the Churches of Christ in the U.S.A. Used by permission. All rights reserved.

Cover and interior design by Think Design Group

ISBN 0-8294-2088-6
International Standard Serial Number (ISSN) 1556-259X

Printed in the United States of America
05 06 07 08 09 10 11 Versa 10 9 8 7 6 5 4 3 2 1

Contents

Introduction

A while ago I shuffled and shambled into the noon Mass at the university where I work, a Mass that is the loveliest loneliest thing most of the time, because usually there are a dozen people there at most, counting the celebrant and the Special Guest who arrives in the middle of the Mass, so there is a real meal feel to it, the sharing of food around a table with people you know but don't know all that well, like second cousins. Plus in summer and fall there are great buttery bars of light falling into the chapel from the high windows, and sometimes there are swallows zooming through Mass because the young priest who runs the chapel likes to leave the doors propped open, and sometimes there is an addled guy who talks to himself the whole Mass and apparently had a really colorful life, at least from what he mutters; and also I never know which of the university's priests or visiting priests will be celebrating the Mass, so every time you go it is a surprise to see who is driving the bus, which is sort of cool, and one of the reasons I go.

There are a lot of other reasons I go, some of them having to do with light and forgiveness and pain and my mom and swallows and my children and peace and the Madonna and addled guys, of which, let's face it, I am one, so I go to Mass at the chapel a lot.

The other day I wander into the chapel at exactly the instant Mass begins, and I sigh to see the celebrant, for it is the university's touchiest testiest most querulous most irascible priest, a guy whose sermons go charging off in ten directions at once, a guy who isn't at all shy about snarling at the congregation, a guy likely to lecture for half an hour on proper attire or how exactly saints were roasted in the good old days when there *were* such creatures as saints, not like *today,* when all he sees are herds of contented *cows* in the chapel and no brave *crusaders* against evil and cant that *he* notices.

But you can't in good conscience tiptoe out of Mass the instant it begins (though you can, technically, tiptoe out of Mass the instant that the bread and wine have been changed into Christ); you have to witness the miracle, that's a given, but leaving because you don't like the celebrant, that's bad form, so I sit down, and Mass begins, and very soon, for the thousandth time in my rumpled life, I am entranced by the simple human genius and theater of the Mass, the way it is a series of stories, a fabric of voices, a braiding of experience and witness, a commitment to the illogical and nonsensical. We have a sliver of bread and a sip of wine and we shake hands. A woman who doesn't sing very well sings two songs, and a man who doesn't read very well aloud reads aloud. It moves me more than I can explain. As I get older it is the small things that seem the biggest to me, and the fact that the singer doesn't sing very well seems unutterably sweet.

During the Mass I notice the testy priest fumbling a bit for his cruets and the right page of the text, and he seems distracted when he gives his (blessedly short and sensible) sermon, and I notice that when he shakes hands he lets people come to him rather than go to them or sprint around the chapel pumping hands, as I saw a young priest do once, but I don't think much about it; he is older than dirt and probably feeling Paleozoic this morning. But then I watch for a moment after the ceremony as he undoes his vestments and puts away book, chalice, clothes; I watch him carefully reaching for things and feeling his way around the room; and I realize he is blind.

I have known this man for years. He is charming, a grouch, brilliant, fascinating, frustrating, petty, generous, and he is also, I now realize, a consummate actor. He has slowly been going blind for years, and because he is prickly proud and wishes to still be of service, he has told no one, and now he is as blind as a door, and I will tell no one.

He shuffles quickly out of the chapel and off to lunch, which he never misses (he never misses any meal whatsoever, but you can't imagine where the food goes, he is skinny as a stick), and I watch him shuffle off down a sidewalk he has used for fifty years, and I turn and go right back into the chapel to ask forgiveness for being such a boneheaded wooden-hearted impatient arrogant mulish stump of a man. I talk to the Madonna for a while, and as usual I do all the talking and herself does all the listening, and then I just sit and watch the buttery bars of light.

I think about the motley chaotic confusing house that is Catholicism. I think about the mad wondrous prayer of the Mass. I think about how there are such stunning and wonderful and confusing people in the clan of Catholics. I think about how we are all several kinds of people at once and hardly know ourselves, let alone anybody else. I think about how *possible* the church is, and how possible we are. I think about how, really, the Church is just lots and lots of us gathered for little holy meals and story swaps. I think about how religions are like people, capable of both extraordinary evil and unimaginable grace. I think about how the church is sort of like the windows above me, which catch these timbers of sun and focus them on the human comedy. I think about how I would be a lot less of a man if I didn't have ways to wake up to what I can be if I harness mercy and humor and wisdom and attention and prayer and humility and courage and grace.

This is what all the stories in this collection are about. This is what all true stories are about, which is what we are, really, at our best—true stories. And true stories, stories with love and power in them, can save your life and save your soul and bring you, if only for a flickering instant, face-to-face with the unimaginable creative force that once, a very long time ago, explained itself to Moses as, simply and confusingly, *I Am Who Am*. That force is in you, in every moment, in every story. Here are some of those stories.

—Brian Doyle

A Note on the Selections

After the first volume of Loyola Press's annual Best Catholic Writing anthology appeared, in the fall of 2004, I was slathered and deluged by letters—paper and electronic—from people intrigued by, curious about, and/or apoplectic over the manner by which such subjective creatures as best Catholic essays or articles or poems were chosen by the editor, who was characterized in some of those letters as brazen, a donkey, a madman, a brave clown, Sisyphus, and suchlike.

And *those* were just the notes from my mama.

Thus this note, to shed a little muddy light on the system.

It is pretty simple: I read everything I can get my paws or ears on—magazines, newspapers, newsletters, blogs, speeches, webzines, scripts, transcripts, songs, books, manuscripts, etc. Some of this material comes to me in the normal course of things, and some of it is sent to me by the editors at Loyola Press, and some more is sent to me by alert and curious readers who join the Best Catholic Writing staff in wanting to share some of this remarkable writing with a way bigger audience than many of these pieces found on first appearance, a desire that is a sort of prayer, really, if you think about it; but a great deal of this material is sent to me over the transom, in the lovely old editorial phrase that no one understands anymore because doors no longer actually *have* transoms, which were the little flaps that opened at the top, remember? Like when you were a kid in school and it was wicked hot, and the teacher would go over to the door and open the transom with a little cranking tool so the flap opened to admit fresh air, but the door stayed closed to prevent the ingress of dogs and principals and pastors and such? Remember?

Well, I can see you *don't* remember, which means you are young and I am Methuselah, but anyway, trust me, magazine editors' offices *used* to have such things through which manuscripts were heaved by the shovelful and from which came the phrase *over the transom,* which means unsolicited, which brings me back to the point at hand, which is to say loudly, I WILL READ ANY AND ALL THINGS SENT TO ME BY YOU AND YOUR FRIENDS AND COMPANIONS AND COLLEAGUES AND FELLOW CONSPIRATORS, if you mail them to me either by post or electronically, to *Portland Magazine,* University of Portland, 5000 North Willamette Boulevard, Portland, OR 97203, bdoyle@up.edu. To be honest, e-mail attachments are probably best.

Or you can send whatever you think would be a good candidate for this series to Jim Manney or Joe Durepos at Loyola Press, 3441 North Ashland Avenue, Chicago, IL 60657, manney@loyolapress.com.

I am also often asked what the criteria are by which a piece is chosen for the anthology. Answer: I can't explain it very well. Generally the pieces with the best chance of being selected are those that are not stuffy, enormous, political, or devout with a capital *D.* The only thing I can easily say is that the best pieces seem *real*—real stories, real emotions and opinions, real maps of the heart.

I should also note that I cheerfully read and sometimes accept pieces from nations other than North America (note the Australian and British writers in this volume); that the very biggest and most controversial subjects are of course meat for this maw (note the articles on war and same-sex marriage and abortion); and that I am fascinated by all forms of storytelling (note the blog excerpt), not just formal essays, although I dearly love essays and consider them the greatest of all literary forms.

But the easiest thing to say is that if you think your piece, or a piece you read, or a piece someone you admire wrote or said or sang, should be in *The Best Catholic Writing 2006*, why, then, just send it along, and let's see.

Remember, too, that Catholic for our purposes absolutely does and should and must mean catholic. Yes, of course, I am interested in pieces by, for, and about Catholics and Catholicism. But it would be a poor mean sniveling driveling frightened little church that did not gaily and grimly seek to grapple with good and evil and grace and greed and courage and cruelty and prayer and passion and sensuality and commerce and war and wine on the largest possible scale, and so you bet we are interested in pieces by, for, and about Buddhists, agnostics, and even Yankees fans. I point out, for example, the amazing essay by the Jewish genius Cynthia Ozick on page 177.

Last notes: the volume of submissions is becoming oceanic, which generally precludes, I am sorry to say, polite notes of demurral from the editor; if your piece is chosen for the 2006 volume, you will be asked if we can rent it, and if it isn't chosen, I thank you right now for having the energy and grace to send it along on its adventure.

And a final note: thanks. For reading this book. For the courage to be Catholic, which is sometimes exhausting and insane-making. For your grace under duress, which is what matters. That and mercy, and humor wherever possible, and being kind and attentive to children. Prayers all around.

—Brian Doyle

The Ordinary Isn't

David Scott

from A Revolution of Love

She did not lead a stirring life. She has no dramatic conversion story. She wasn't knocked off a horse and blinded by a brilliant light from heaven, as St. Paul was. We find in her story none of the high sexual drama that Augustine confessed. There is none of the shuttle diplomacy of Bridget of Sweden or Catherine of Siena. Unlike Thomas More, she didn't have her head chopped off.

Her story is ostensibly simple: She became a nun at age eighteen and some years later was riding on a train when she heard a voice telling her to leave her religious order to serve the poor. So that's what she did until she died.

Her work wasn't all that exceptional, especially for a nun. Plenty of people do what she did—take care of the sick and dying, find homes for abandoned children, defend the poor, the unwanted, the unborn. "There was nothing otherworldly or divine about her," said the musician Bob Geldof, who met her in Ethiopia, and his opinion is echoed again and again. In spite of all the photographs and books and fame and prizes, in spite of the fact that Pope John Paul II not only beatified her immediately but reportedly had to be persuaded against rushing to canonize her, we don't actually know much about the person. Who *was* Mother Teresa?

Here is what we know: She was born Gonxha Agnes on August 26, 1910, in Skopje, Macedonia. She was the youngest of three children born to Nikola and Drana Bojaxhiu. She was an Albanian Catholic, born in the year of a great Albanian uprising, and during her first years, her home city was invaded by Serbians who spent days on an ethnic raid—raping, torturing, and murdering her neighbors and kin.

Her father was a successful merchant and investor who served on the town council and was often out of the country on business. But Nikola's passion was Albanian independence: he hosted political strategy sessions in his home and apparently helped bankroll the movement to establish an Albanian state in the Kosovo region. That is supposedly what got him killed. At a political fund-raising dinner in 1919, he was poisoned, presumably by vengeful Yugoslavian authorities.

After Nikola's death, his business partners grabbed his share of everything and ran, leaving the Bojaxhius in financial straits. Drana supported the family by sewing and making rugs. She went to Mass daily at the Church of the Sacred Heart down the street, brought food to the poor, opened the family dinner table to the homeless, and gave refuge to women in need. "We had guests at table every day," remembered Teresa. "At first I used to ask: 'Who are they?' and Mother would answer: 'Some are our relatives, but all of them are our people.' When I was older, I realized that the strangers were poor people who had nothing."

Teresa seems to have been a serious, bookish, and sickly girl, prone to whooping cough and other infections. She loved music, played a mean piano and mandolin, wrote poetry, acted in plays. She sang in the church choir and led a girls' society devoted to the Virgin Mary. Attracted by what she had read of their work in India, she decided to join the Sisters of Loreto. When Teresa told her mother, Drana locked herself in her room and didn't come out for a day. When she finally emerged, she said to her daughter, "Put your hand in his . . . and walk all the way with him." Gonxha set sail for India in late 1928 and never saw her mother again.

Mother Teresa gave us next to nothing of her own story, and we should wonder why. She lived in our times of utter revelation, and yet her personal life is a closed book. You might say her first miracle was living in this age but flying beneath the radar, preserving her zone of personal privacy. Would-be muckrakers stumbled in their own muck. There were no whistle-blowers, no believable tales told out of school by disgruntled former coworkers. Even the forces of nature behaved as if carrying out some unspoken mandate: when an earthquake leveled her childhood home and neighborhood in 1963, it was like a divine conversation-stopper, God forever interring her past in rubble and ruin.

We are left without a clue, except for one thing: her name. In an instance of self-disclosure so rare that we should take notice, she made her official biographers report that she took the name of St. Thérèse of Lisieux and *not* St. Teresa of Ávila. "Not the big St. Teresa but the little one," she said, without further explanation. So she took the name of a bourgeois girl who entered a Carmelite convent at fifteen and spent her days praying, doing the laundry, and accomplishing so little of moment that a fellow nun worried aloud that Thérèse would be hard to eulogize at her funeral, as "she has certainly never done anything worth speaking of."

However, Thérèse was asked by her mother superior to write her life story, which she dutifully did, expressing in simple language her philosophy of life, which came to be called the "little way"—living with a childlike sense of wonder at God's gifts, with a child's sense of dependence and trust. It meant, Thérèse said, finding the true divine significance "in the least action done out of love."

Published a year after her death, the book became a surprise best seller. It was translated into countless languages and catapulted Thérèse to the ranks of the most beloved and important saints ever. Canonizing her between the world wars, at a time of social unrest and uncertainty, Pope Pius XI declared that if everyone followed her little way, "the reformation of human society would be easily realized." Years later, Pope Pius XII called her "the greatest saint of modern times."

This was the saint Gonxha chose as her patron. Not the big Teresa, the bold reformer and mystic who mapped the soul's interior mansions, landing herself in hot water with the Spanish Inquisition. Gonxha chose the little way. Is there a lesson for us in that choice? Is there a lesson in the holiness of the ordinary, in the divine in the routine, in the idea that God comes to us not as a bolt out of the blue but in the din of the day, in families and workplaces, in struggles and joys, in the people he puts in our path, in the trials and sufferings he sends our way?

Subshasini Das came to Mother Teresa in 1949 during the first days of Teresa's ministry on the streets of Calcutta. A privileged Bengali girl, Das presented herself decked out in jewels and a fine dress and said she wanted to give her life to the poor.

"You must first forget yourself, so that you can dedicate yourself to God and your neighbor," said Teresa, perhaps thinking of John the Baptist: "I must decrease so that Jesus might increase."

Das returned after weeks of soul-searching, clad in a plain white robe. She went on to become the first nun in Mother Teresa's new religious order, the Missionaries of Charity.

You must first forget yourself, said Teresa to a narcissistic generation, to people self-occupied yet still strangers to themselves. She watched patiently as wave after wave of young women and men shucked off their parents' Christianity and turned their hearts east, following some star they thought was rising, some new wisdom they thought would save them from the phoniness and soullessness of their consumer-material world.

"People come to India," she would say, "because they believe that in India we have a lot of spirituality, and this they want to find. . . . Many of them are completely lost."

But for Mother Teresa, detachment and self-denial were not the end goals of our striving; we struggle against selfishness in order to purify our vision, to see, to love.

"Once we take our eyes away from ourselves," she said, "from our interests, from our own rights, privileges, ambitions—then we will become clear to see Jesus around us," she promised. In every face, in every heart, in every moment.

One of the lost seekers who crossed her path was Morris Siegel. In 1969, he launched an herbal tea company, Celestial Seasonings, that caught the first wave of the all-natural, organic health craze and rode it all the way to the bank. By 1985, he had sold his company for forty million dollars and was desperately seeking meaning. He showed up as a volunteer at Mother Teresa's Home for the Destitute Dying. She poked him in the chest and sent him home with these words: "Grow where you're planted."

It's so easy to love people we don't know, so easy that it is no love at all. We like love in the abstract—love of the poor, the sick, the handicapped—but we're afraid of close-ups, the flesh-and-blood poor people and sick people, the family members and friends whom God plants in our midst. "It is easier to give a cup of rice to relieve hunger than to relieve the loneliness and pain of someone unloved in our own home.

Bring love into your home. . . . The world today is upside down, and is suffering so much, because there is so very little love in the homes. . . . We have not time for our children; we have not time for each other."

She came slowly to the work that would define her. From 1929, when she landed in Calcutta, until 1947, she lived and worked mostly within the insular confines of St. Mary's School, a primly landscaped, high-walled campus run by the Loreto Sisters. She spent her days teaching history and geography to girls from colonial India's professional and political classes. Had she wanted to, she could have looked beyond the walls and down upon one of Calcutta's worst *bustees*, or slums: Motijhil, or "Pearl Lake," named ironically for the foul pond in the center of the teeming maze of mud alleyways and shacks that were home to thousands of the poor.

A group of girls from her school, led by its Jesuit chaplain, visited Motijhil every Sunday, bringing food and doing some charitable works. Mother Teresa never went with them. In fact, during her years as a teacher and later as principal of the school, she never said or did anything about the poor that anyone can remember.

Her hour had not yet come, say her biographers, lamely.

But then her hour did come. On August 16, 1946, the world crashed up against the walls of St. Mary's, and Mother Teresa could ignore it no longer. Mob violence between Muslims and Hindus put the compound under virtual siege, and she was driven out in a desperate search for food for the three hundred girls in her care. What she saw made her blood run cold: fires burning inside shattered storefronts; human remains splattered on and dripping down brick walls; bodies and parts of bodies strewn everywhere—on sidewalks, in gutters, on roads; vultures picking bones. Five thousand people were killed that day; fifteen thousand were wounded.

Less than one month later, on September 10, 1946, Mother Teresa was riding the train from Calcutta to Darjeeling, on her way to make her annual retreat, when she heard a voice speaking in her heart, as she later described it. It was Jesus telling her to quit the convent to live and work with the poor. For the rest of her life she ducked every inquiry about that voice. She would say only that she was sure it was Jesus and that his message was unmistakable.

"It was an order," she said.

After she died, a small cache of her letters was found— letters written to her spiritual directors and superiors during her early years. In one, to Ferdinand Périer, a Jesuit who was archbishop of Calcutta, she describes the Voice she heard on the train and in the days and weeks that followed.

"I want Indian Missionary Sisters of Charity, who would be My fire of love amongst the very poor—the sick, the dying, the little street children," Jesus told her. "The poor I want you to bring to Me. . . . Come, come, carry Me into the holes of the poor, . . . their dark, unhappy homes. . . . You are, I know, the most incapable person, weak and sinful, but just because you are that, I want to use you for My glory! Wilt thou refuse!"

Go to the poor she did. On August 17, 1948, she walked out beyond the walls of St. Mary's wearing a plain white sari. She had five rupees in her pocket. She took a short course in basic medicine, found a place to live in a convent of the Little Sisters of the Poor, and began her work. She started by teaching the alphabet to poor children in classes she conducted under a plum tree in the middle of the slums. Soon she was going from hovel to hovel, visiting the children's families, bringing them food and conversation. One by one, former students joined her in the work. By 1950, this group of women was recognized by the church as an official religious order, the Missionaries of Charity, now working in more than thirty countries.

"We have a terrible hunger for God," Teresa said. "We have been created to be loved. . . . He makes Himself the hungry one, not only for bread, but for love. He makes Himself the naked one, not only for a piece of cloth but for that understanding love, that dignity, human dignity. He makes Himself the homeless one, not only for the piece of a small room, but for that deep sincere love for the other. And this is the Eucharist."

For her, our failure to see Christ in the beggar was a sign that we had lost our ability to find him in the Eucharist. We might think we believe these things, but we are wrong. We are playing out the mystery recorded in the Gospel—of Jesus coming into the world and not being recognized as God. "Today, as before, when Jesus comes amongst His own, His own don't know Him," she said. "He comes in the rotting bodies of the poor. . . . Jesus comes to you and me. And often, very often, we pass Him by."

St. John Chrysostom put it this way: "Do you wish to honor the body of Christ? Do not ignore Him when He is naked. Do not pay Him homage in the temple clad in silk only then to neglect Him outside where He suffers cold and nakedness."

Teresa insisted, in a way that no saint ever had, that our salvation is bound up in some mysterious way with our love of the poor. "The poor are the hope of . . . the people of America, for in them we see the hungry Christ looking up at us. Will we refuse Him?"

"Mother Teresa takes care of the poorest of the poor but never deals with why they are poor," a charities official for the British Catholic bishops once complained. "We are fighting for justice," said another Briton, and she "deals only with the disease [of poverty] and not with preventing it. But people in the West continue to give her money." She did refuse to point fingers at ruthless dictators, corrupt politicians, and multinational corporate bandits. She did meet with them and accept donations from them and suffer being called a chaplain to the rich.

Her critics were right, of course. She had nothing of substance to show for half a century of work with the poor. The poor were poor and badly treated in Calcutta before she arrived, and they are poor and badly treated still today. The same is true in every other country where her nuns have set up shop. Still, her critics' picture of her was a caricature. She did criticize the arms race in the third world as theft from the poor; she did decry the avarice and greed that enabled some nations to live high on the hog while others barely survived; she did denounce rich nations forcing birth control, abortion, and sterilization on the poor; she did appeal to world leaders on behalf of refugees and victims of war; she was vocal against the death penalty, euthanasia, and abortion. But she had no illusions that revolution or a change of political parties would improve the lot of the poor. She never faulted those working to nonviolently change political institutions and economic structures. She, however, heard a different call. She worked from below. "There are thousands and thousands of poor, but I think of only one at a time," she said. "Jesus was only one, and I take Jesus at His word. . . .You can save only one at a time. We can only love one at a time."

Once, in London, she was walking down the street and came upon a drunk man. She took him by the hand, looked into his eyes, and asked him how he was doing. His face lit up. "Oh, after so long I feel the warmth of a human hand," he said.

She will forever be remembered as Mother Teresa of Calcutta: a Christian holy woman in the city named for the Hindu goddess Kali.

To help Mother Teresa start her home for the dying, Calcutta's city fathers gave her an abandoned building attached to one of Hinduism's most revered Kali shrines. No doubt they congratulated themselves on finding her an eminently practical location; the building was joined to Kalighat, near a municipal funeral pyre where day and night the bodies of the dead are wrapped in white linen and consigned to the flames, their ashes scattered in the Hooghly River, which flows into the sacred Ganges.

It was a good plan. The destitute could come to Mother Teresa's to die and could then be carted over to the crematory for the disposition of their mortal remains.

How interesting that Mother Teresa's home for the dying wound up alongside a shrine to Kali—"the Black One," the giver of all life and the one who takes it all away. Idols of Kali are terrifying; black as soot, eyes wild, tongue lolling and dripping with blood, she wears a necklace of freshly severed human heads, carries a cleaver and a noose, and is posed in a feverish dance. Kali priests are said to have murdered the first Christian missionary to India, running the doubting apostle St. Thomas through with a spear in the year 72. Deep into the nineteenth century, Kali worship often entailed human sacrifice, and even today Kali priests offer her blood sacrifices, from the slit throats of black goats.

Mother Teresa never said a word publicly about Kali or her cult. Teresa named her home for the destitute dying Nirmal Hriday, "Place of the Immaculate Heart," in honor of Mary. It was a blunt contrast, to say the least: the image of the gentle mother alongside the violent mother. Was Mother Teresa lobbing a potshot at her Hindu neighbors, making a wry slur against their goddess? They probably thought so at first. In the early days of Nirmal Hriday, angry mobs, whipped up by the temple priests, staged protests and made death threats against Mother Teresa, accusing her of a stealth campaign to convert Hindus. That all ended when she took in and nursed one of her most virulent enemies, a young Kali priest who was dying of tuberculosis and had been denied care by the city's hospitals.

That was her way. She viewed the world as caught up in an apocalyptic struggle between maternal love and a dark, demonic perversion of motherhood. In the divine script of her life, Mother Teresa of Calcutta was based alongside Kali's cultic center to illuminate this clash of worldviews. She was not sent into the world to offer Catholic commentary on Hindu deities or devotions. Far more was at stake than any superficial concerns for religious tolerance and diversity. She was sent at a post-Christian moment in history, when Western societies were in the process of rejecting and moving beyond two thousand years of beliefs, values, and assumptions based on the teachings of Christ. In moving beyond Christianity the world was actually sliding back into paganism—the shape of religion before revelation, before God chose to make his covenant with Abraham and to show us his face in Jesus.

Without ever using the word, Mother Teresa showed us the new paganism of our post-Christian world. In the West, the fervid orgies of fertility cults had been replaced by an idolatrous glorification of sex. In place of ancient child sacrifices were a state-sanctioned cult of abortion and the "assisted suicide" of the weak. The new paganism she prophesied against was a sort of secular religion promoted by multinational corporations, rulers of nations, and international agencies.

Mother Teresa surprised even longtime supporters when she devoted her Nobel Peace Prize acceptance speech to abortion, which she described as the "greatest destroyer of peace today." Her colleagues had prepped her to talk about the nuclear arms race and neoimperialism in the third world. The diplomats who had nominated her for the prize came expecting tales of uplift from her work among the poor and dying.

Instead she spoke from the heart about a Kaliesque issue: "a direct war, a direct killing—direct murder by the mother herself." For her, abortion was the mother of all problems, of all violence, of all poverty. "Nations who destroy life by abortion and euthanasia are the poorest," she said. "For they have not got food for one more child, a home for one old person. So they must add one more cruel murder into this world."

If a mother is permitted to kill her baby, she said, everything must be permitted, every violence expected. "We must not be surprised when we hear of murders, of killings, of wars. If a mother can kill her own child, what is left but for us to kill each other? I do not want to talk about what should be legal or illegal. I do not think any human heart should dare to take life, or any human hand be raised to destroy life. Life is the life of God in us, even in an unborn child."

After 1946, we now know, Mother Teresa only once more heard the voice of God, and she believed the doors of heaven had been closed and bolted against her. The more she longed for some sign of his presence, the emptier and more desolate she became. We always saw her smiling. She had a playful smile, mischievous, as if she was privy to some secret joke. Especially when she was around children, she beamed with delight. In private, she had a quick, self-deprecating sense of humor and sometimes doubled over from laughing so hard. So many people who spent time with her came away saying that she was the most joyful person they had ever met.

But we know that in secret her life was a living hell. She confided to her spiritual director in 1957, "I call, I cling, I want, and there is no one to answer. . . . The reality of emptiness is so great that nothing touches my soul." As if by some strange formula, the greater her success and public adulation, the more abandoned, humiliated, and desperate she felt. "I feel like refusing God," she wrote.

In her dark night we can hear all the anguish of our time: the desolation of the poor, the cries of unwanted children—of all those who cannot bring themselves to pray or to love. We hear . . . us. But what we see is a tiny smiling woman who did not refuse the Voice she heard on the train one day.

She died on September 5, 1997, a great apostle of joy and light in the dark final hours of the second Christian millennium. She died almost one hundred years to the day after her patron Thérèse of the little way. She died as one of the century's great living expressions of love for children. She died as, perhaps, the first bud of a new Christian life, flowering from the bloody soil of the most murderous century in history.

The French Guy

David James Duncan

from *Portland Magazine*

I was recently asked by Earth Ministry of Seattle to speak on the feast day of St. Francis, October 4. In preparing that talk, I thought it appropriate to say a few words about what sort of man Francis "really was." In trying to capture the Assisian on paper, however, I met with near-complete literary failure.

My failure began with research and notes. I noted, for example, that he was not named Francis. He was named John by his parents, Peter and Pica Bernardone of Assisi, but Peter spent so much time on the road, enriching his already rich self, that he was off trading in France when his son was born, causing mischievous neighbors to nick his son's name to *Francesco,* which basically means "the French guy."

I researched the saint online and found some distressingly cuddly Web sites that called Francis stuff like "the father of the ecology movement." I couldn't see this at all. Francis, for all his love of nature, was consumed not by any kind of ecology but by burning love for Jesus Christ. Francis was not an activist or a contemplative per se, but an *active contemplative* who could conduct his outer life at full speed without his inner life being overwhelmed or lost. He was also a nonintellectual and a terrible literalist. To wit:

Because Jesus said, "Give everything to the poor and follow me," Francis gave away his home, parents, dignity, lute, hat with the cool feather, and clothes and stood naked as a baby in the public square;

And because Genesis said that God made and blessed all creatures, plants, landforms, and elements, Francis loved them all, including wolves, lizards, snakes, blizzards, volcanoes, rain and lightning storms, and every creepy crawly biting stinging insect, plant, or human on earth, *especially* those that attacked, and so in his view blessed, the person of Francis himself;

And because the Son of Man had no place to lay his head, Francis refused to own property of any kind, including even sandals to negotiate the stone terrain of Umbria, and so spent his life bare and bloody-footed, which is to say "blessed" by all those stones.

What most of us might consider our imaginative or prayer or inner lives Francis considered his vivid, immediate, physical life. The visible body of his boon companion, Jesus, for instance, left this world some twelve hundred years before Francis was even born, a distance that would reduce lesser men and women to a relationship consisting chiefly of prayer, hymns, or the recitation of old Bible stories. Francis, however, not only prayed and sang to and told stories about Jesus, he also talked with and danced for and bowed and babbled to him like nothing we have seen except the street mad and bag ladies, really—thanking Christ for every blow received at the hands of thugs, every insult from skeptics and mockers, every pang of hunger, every turn of the weather (especially turns for the ever-blessed worse), every scrap of begged food.

But even old Francis had a body. And in and of itself, this body was a comfort-loving animal, like our own. And there were times in his long marriage to poverty when his animal body hadn't eaten for days, or even weeks, and was literally starving, so that when Francis and his brothers finally begged a little food, and got lucky enough to cook it, it smelled so marvelous that, upon bowing over it, even in Christ's presence, poor Francis's eyes would crave the food not only because it was the gift of Christ but because *dang* it smelled *good!* and he was stark raving starvin'! Any "ecologist" I know would thank the earth for its bounty in such a circumstance and devour the food with utmost happiness. But when this kind of feeling rose in the Assisian saint, his heart stopped him on a dime, *errt!,* stood him up, and sent him to the nearest stove or campfire, where he'd grab fistfuls of ashes, return to his lovely food, and sling them on.

Why oh why? Perhaps because food topped with ashes is darned hard for mind and body to desire. And "in desirelessness," said the excommunicated Saint Meister Eckhart, "is the virgin that eternally gives birth to the Son." Having preserved this virginity and this birth, Francis lit into his meal with gooey-, gray-mouthed relish.

I felt awe for a while about all of this. But as Francis's Christ-loving deeds multiplied and the desperation of deed deepened, it occurred to me, in the animal comfort of my study, clothing, socks, and shoes, that to give a man as average as me a chance to speak of a man as sublimely love crazed as Francis is to give that average man a chance to sound like a high-flown platitudinous ninny. Francis's love for his Lord was so ecstatic, creative, physical, and contagious that even though there are things I believe I would die for, I feel, in comparison to this man, that I have hardly begun to love at all. As far as I can see, Francis had no "average" or "everyday" sense of things at all: for him every creature was a miracle, every moment a gift, every breath a prayer in God's Presence, and if we were sitting with him tonight disbelieving in his miracles, gifts, and

Presence completely, he'd go on believing in them so much more powerfully than us bums know how to disbelieve that we would have to run from the room to escape the great gravitational pull of his love.

Feeling of all this, I suddenly felt so lamely literary, so papery, inky, and abstract, that I did something strange: with all the love for the French guy I could muster, I abandoned my computer and office, marched to the kitchen, grabbed a teaspoon, took it in the living room, opened the woodstove, dug out a heaping teaspoonful of cold ashes, and—hoping to learn at least the flavor, if not the feeling, that Francis once knew well—shoved it in my mouth.

Guess what?

The taste wasn't as shocking as I'd feared—at first. Woodstove ashes taste the same way they smell—at first. But the mouth encloses this taste so completely, and your taste buds and salivary glands then greet it so confusedly, that the encounter intensifies, soon taking you places well beyond anything you could detect from the smell. Ashes taste, after you've worked them around in your mouth awhile, like a message from somewhere far from this life. The literary part of me wants to say something like "Ashes taste like the most incinerated piece of sixth-circle *infernal bowge meat* Dante ever imagined!" But ashes taste like something beyond the literary part of me. A lot of my dear friends and family are ashes today. I began to taste them in the ashes—yet the taste did not sadden me. If I were to put a single word on the flavor in my mouth, I would say it was that of *finality,* which has something in common with eternity; and what eternity is to time, infinity is to space—and as the great Hindu scriptures, the Upanishads, long ago put it: "There is no joy in the finite. There is joy only in the Infinite." This joy source, I believe, is why Francis threw ashes on every animal pleasure: he was not a killjoy; he was joy's greatest lover, choosing, each time he threw ashes on the wondrous flavors of food, a life of no joy but infinite soul-joy. This equation is way past me. Yet the next thing I knew, I felt joy rising in me not despite, but because of, the spoonful of finality/dead friends/eternity/infinity I had shoved in my mouth.

But woodstove ashes come in extremely dry, powdery form. And the taste of joy was so surprising to me that though I didn't quite gasp, I did draw in a sharp breath—and so inhaled a whole cloud of ash and commenced to cough my lungs out. I spent the next few minutes at the kitchen sink, discovering that it is surprisingly hard to wash the deep gray color and finality flavor of *ashes* off your tongue and your gums. I also had a stomachache for reasons I hope the chemists reading this will keep to themselves.

But I say this, with finality: there will never be an end to Francis's and your and my and every living earthling's relationship with the beauty, finality, eternity, and infinity of regular, normal, there-they-sit-under-everything ashes. Never. And I taste in this seemingly hard fact a grayish-tongued, paradoxical, yet undeniable hint of joy.

Three Poems

Pattiann Rogers

from *Generations*

I. God and His People

He must measure the average
length of the fangs and each claw
unsheathed, calculate the reach
of the forelimbs, the maximum
expanse of the leap.

By sleeping on the grasses
of their abandoned beds, he can become
accustomed to the smothering odors
of their fur and hide, learn to anticipate
the sudden dizzying musk of their resonant
bodies and thereby hope to maintain
equilibrium in their presence.

The clever feint and dodge, the pistol
loaded with blanks, the report of the whip
snapped in midair will often stay

a treachery. Fire of candle or small torch
thrust quickly forward by surprise
may momentarily keep desertion at bay.
Not one must be damaged.

He attends to the plaint of their roarings—
how the sound imitates in possibility
the breadth of the starry savannah,
in certainty the thunderous sky
of wildebeests in stampede. He must read
and absorb the entire vocal range
of their rages and victories, the lesser
growls and spittings of their lovemaking.

Here are the bones, the blackened blood
left from their feedings. All of them
eat flesh and lick the leavings.

Perhaps they will sit still on their small
stools and wait, watching him. Perhaps
they will saunter snarling in a line
around the ring and stop to rise reluctantly
on their hind legs before him, meet
his eyes, imitate prayer.

If the nuance of the fake charge
is mastered, if the dance of the tail
is interpreted, if the prophecy of pant
and crouch is forsworn, then the time
may arrive when pity will appear among them
and the door of the cage open, and he will
step out, released and resurrected.

II. Gehenna

Throw them into the pit, dump
them all in, the sacks of bones
and baskets of ashes, shovel in
the shards, the dusty chaff, corn
shucks, potsherds, smoking clinkers,
piles of snuffed candle stubs.

In they go, bundles of oily rags
and nappies, caskets of poxy
bedclothes, tattered burlap bags
of spent shells, armless dolls
and wheelless wheelbarrows,
the stripped spokes of slaughtered
umbrellas, everything bulldozed in,
cracked cups and dented kettles,
tarnished brass bells without clappers,
ball joints, steering columns and bent
axles, wagonloads of smoldering
tires, crushed hubcaps, the half
hulls of bottomless boats.

Haul them over and push them in,
carcasses of bedsprings, stained
velvet sofas and overstuffed chairs
spilling stuffing, splintered tables,
smashed pianos, scorched shoes
and burnt brooms, tangles of chains,
handcuffs and busted locks,
buckets of rusty wires, nails, bolts,
leaking batteries, empty paint cans,

frozen hinges and headless hammers.
Up to the edge, over the side,
into the pit, shove them in, all away.
There they go catapulting
and crashing down, a continuous
clattering racket thundering
dust and reeking smoke of tar,
one odd ping of a piano string,
a few brief flames spitting
and hissing, the entire roaring
mischief falling away, down,
dimming, deeper, farther.

A hollow of quiet begins to rise
as the clanking tumult vanishes
into the depths, beyond sight,
beyond sound, maybe beyond
the moon beyond the planets,
maybe beyond motion itself, past
the midway to everything else.
And I know for certain
salvation exists. Beautiful,
blessed pit.

III. A Statement of Certainty

Here we are, all of us now, some of us
in emerald feathers, in chestnut or purple,
some with bodies of silver, red,
or azure scales, some with faces
of golden fur, some with sea-floating
sails of translucent blue, some pulsing

with fluorescence at dusk, some
pulsing inside shell coverings shining
like obsidian, or inside whorled
and spotted spindle shells, or inside
leaves and petals folded and sealed
like tender shells.

Because many of us have many names—
black-masked or black-footed or blue-
footed, spiny, barbed, whiskered, or ringed,
three-toed, nine-banded, four-horned,
whistling or piping, scavenger or prey—
we understand this attribute of god.
Because some of us, not yet found, possess
no names of any kind, we understand,
as well, this attribute of god.

All of us are here, whether wingless
clawless, eyeless, or legless, voiceless,
or motionless, whether hanging
as pods of fur and breath in branches
knitted over the earth or hanging
from stone ceilings in mazes of hallways
beneath the earth, whether blown across
oceans trailing tethers of silk, or taken
off course, caught in storms of thunder
currents or tides of snow, whether free
in cells of honey or free over tundra
plains or alive inside the hearts of living
trees, whether merely moments of inert
binding in the tight blink of buried
eggs, or a grip of watching in the cold
wick of water-swept seeds, this—beyond
faith, beyond doubt—we are here.

Meeting Father Zhang

Emily Wu

from *America*

"We are going to have a French teacher!"

I grabbed Rui Yin's arm excitedly and whispered as I sat down. It had been her turn to wait and fight for the precious few library seats. She was sturdily built and could usually push through the crowd of students waiting for the library door to open at 7:30 PM. On that humid and hot evening in 1979, we were sophomores majoring in English at Anhui Teachers University in Wuhu City, China.

We had to learn a second foreign language in order to graduate. Rui Yin and I had signed up for French, but for more than a year the university had not been able to find a teacher.

"Really?" she screamed.

"Shh. You are getting us kicked out." I caught the annoyed glances from those sitting around us and wrote on my notebook for her: "I went home for dinner. Party Secretary Ling was asking my father to test this French teacher tomorrow. My father said that he was an English professor. She said that it didn't matter because he was the only one who knew any French."

The next Tuesday morning, we anxiously awaited our first French lesson. A frail old hunchback with pure white hair walked slowly into the classroom. He stood quietly at the podium, staring down at the ground.

The students looked at one another, not knowing what to make of the new teacher's behavior. After a few minutes, he opened his mouth to say something, but the words disappeared before they reached his throat. Two strings of tears rolled slowly down his wrinkled cheeks like pearls.

"Stu . . . dents," he stuttered, "for . . . give me . . . for . . . talking . . . like . . . this. I . . . have . . . not talked . . . to . . . humans . . . for . . . almost . . . thirty . . . years. My . . . last . . . name . . . is . . . Zhang." He wiped off the tears with his sleeve and bowed.

The classroom was so quiet that I heard a lone cricket chirping outside. Someone asked timidly, "Teacher Zhang, who have you been talking to, then?"

"God," he said. The students burst into laughter. Religion of any kind, especially Catholicism, had been purged since the Communist takeover in 1949. It was the first time we had heard anyone say the word *God* in a serious tone.

"Where have you been talking to God?" someone else asked, somewhat mockingly.

"Pri . . . son" was his labored answer.

"Ah . . . " We were taken aback and remained silent for the rest of class.

I found out later that Zhang had gone to prison because he was a Catholic priest. He had been locked up in a single cell for almost all of those years. His belief in God kept him alive. He was assigned a teaching post at our university after he got out of prison.

His French, learned some forty years ago, was almost forgotten. He would often stop in midsentence, trying to remember a word or phrase. Nevertheless, nobody complained about his teaching.

I developed a special admiration for him. My mother was the youngest of eight children. Her brother and sister introduced her to Catholicism in 1946.

My third uncle was a famous historian who specialized in religious studies. In 1952 he was tortured and kept in a cell so small that he could only sit.

My second aunt was a promising twenty-six-year-old medical student when she went to prison in 1951 for her belief. She stayed in a single cell for about the same length of time as Teacher Zhang. In those solitary years, she took apart a knit white sock, knotted the threads into a rosary, and prayed.

After second aunt's arrest, my grandmother wept day and night until she nearly went blind. Even when she was dying of cancer in 1964, they didn't have a chance to meet for one last time.

My fourth uncle was not a Catholic. In 1966, the Red Guards accused him of being a secret Catholic priest, beating him terribly in an attempt to make him confess to a nonexistent crime.

He escaped and tried to commit suicide by jumping into the Yellow River. A fisherman pulled him ashore. The Red Guards were furious. They forced my uncle to sit in a chair and hit big iron nails through his palms. Eventually, he went insane.

My mother maintained her belief in God. When my father was sent to prison for criticizing the regime at the Institute of International Relations in Beijing, she told the authorities that persecuting my father was like killing Jesus on the cross.

A few weeks after Zhang arrived, my father was fully rehabilitated as a professor of English. My mother and younger brother moved back to Beijing with him. The day before they left, Mom took me aside.

"Maomao, keep this." She pressed her string of rosary beads into my hands. We had never talked about religion, but I knew she was Catholic. Her rosary was the only religious item she had been able to save after the Red Guards ransacked our apartment too many times. Religious activities took place only secretly in China, and it was not possible to buy the Bible or any other religious items. She hid the rosary in a section of a broken bamboo broom handle.

"Mom, you keep it."

She patted my hands without a word. I put it carefully in my pocket.

A few months later, Zhang was diagnosed with liver cancer. I went to see him in the hospital with several classmates. It was a warm and clear autumn day. Falling leaves danced in the wind and landed by the sidewalk to rot.

He looked pale. The little that remained of his white hair lay loosely on the pillow. We did not know what to say and just stood by his bedside for a while. As soon as we were out of the room, Rui Yin and I started to cry. We knew that it might be the last visit.

"I left my book in his room. I will run to fetch it and catch up with you," I said once we were on the street.

Back at his room, I closed the door behind me and knelt by his bedside. I took out the rosary beads and slowly pressed them into his hand.

"Father Zhang . . ." I couldn't hold back my tears.

"Oh . . ." There was a spark of excitement in his eyes, tears sinking into the pillow. "Are . . . you . . . a . . . Catholic?"

"My mother is. Please keep this."

"God . . . bless . . . you, my . . . child." He lifted the back of his shaking hand toward my face. The distended veins on his hands looked like those on dry leaves.

For more than twenty years, I have been haunted by his image. I wonder what made him and all other Catholics in China endure those years of suffering. Is there a God?

I finally decided to find out last year. I started participating in the Rite of Christian Initiation of Adults. I learned, among other things, that Father Zhang had meant for me to kiss his hand that day, as in a Catholic ceremony. All he received then were drops of my tears.

I will be baptized this Easter.

May I kiss your hand when we meet again, Father Zhang?

A Ghost in the Family

Rod Dreher

from *The Dallas Morning News*

The first time I met the exorcist, he and his helpers were off to clean out, so to speak, a haunted house north of New Orleans. I went with them, saw bizarre things I could not explain, wrote a newspaper story about it, and figured I'd never see those people again.

Two years later, in August of 1994, I phoned the exorcist myself. "Can you come to my mom and dad's house?" I asked. "We buried my grandfather a couple of days ago, and some strange things are going on."

"Day after tomorrow," the exorcist promised. "When we get there, don't tell Shelby your grandfather died. We don't want to lead her in any direction."

I have never been able to forget what happened next. I have thought a lot about it over the past decade, and I am no closer to solving the mysteries at the heart of those events. I can say this for certain: the barrier between the world of the living and the realm of the dead is permeable, and the refusal to recognize the reality of the supernatural can lead to our destruction.

It's one thing to believe this by faith. It's another to see evidence of it with your own eyes.

In 1976, my father's mother died. My grandfather, Murphy, was emotionally devastated, yet within a year he told us he was going to marry again, to an elderly widow I'll call Agnes. The family was startled by this, but the family physician told us that if Murphy didn't have companionship, he would probably lose his will to live. We accepted Agnes into the family, and that was that.

In 1992, I was living in Washington, D.C., and my father phoned from south Louisiana with shocking news. Murphy and Agnes, both now in their eighties, had entered the hospital at the same time for treatment and asked my dad to pay their bills while they were away. Dad decided to audit their accounts and discovered that from virtually the beginning of their marriage, Agnes had been stealing money from my grandfather and putting it into her private account. She had taken about one hundred thousand dollars.

My father, who had limited power of attorney, moved what he could of that money back to Murphy's account, and when the couple returned home, my father confronted them with the facts. He played for me a tape recording of what Agnes shouted at him in that meeting: "If you don't put that money back, you can take this old man home with you right now."

She was shameless enough to say that in front of Murphy. Perhaps because he was starting to go senile, or perhaps because he couldn't grasp that his wife would admit to those feelings, Murphy took her side against my father and ordered him to put the money back. It broke my dad's heart.

There was a lot more heartbreak to come for my dad. He could have disobeyed his father and gone to court to have him declared incompetent, thus saving what was to my grandfather, a retired factory worker, a small fortune. But to do so would have shamed the old man in our small town, and perhaps earned my dad the everlasting enmity of his own father. That he could not risk.

Dad not only put the money back, but he also continued to take care of Murphy's needs, especially driving him to the hospital for his routine cancer treatments, with Agnes riding shotgun in acrid silence. This continued until August of 1994, when my grandfather died on his hospital bed, his iron grip on his son's hand slackening slowly, slowly, until he was gone. My mother phoned me in Washington, and I was on the first flight home.

We had Murphy's funeral at the Methodist church, and after a luncheon at a cousin's house, I returned to Mom and Dad's with them. I sat in my old bedroom, writing on the computer, when suddenly I heard a sharp rapping on the window behind me. I went to see who was there but found no one. The noise was too direct and rhythmic to be that of a bird, and because my parents live out in the country, there would have been no neighbors around to knock on the glass. Not knowing what to make of it, I said nothing.

The next day, my father said to me, "The strangest thing happened last night. I was sitting in my chair in the living room reading. The rest of you were asleep. I heard this rapping running along the side of the house. I went outside to see what was going on. The dogs were sleeping."

Now this was strange. Those dogs bark whenever a deer walks along the edge of the yard. That they would sleep through someone knocking on the windows in the living room was inexplicable.

"I sat back down in the chair and picked up my book," my father continued. "Then I heard the door to our bedroom open and close, and at the end of the hallway I saw a figure in white. I thought it was your mother. I said, 'Honey, is that you?' No answer. I put my glasses on, turned the light on in the hall, and went to check on her. Your mom was sleeping as soundly as ever."

My father is a sensible man, a small-town Methodist not given to hoodoo speculation. I am a Catholic convert who had in recent years been cavorting in the bayous with an exorcist priest who dealt with the paranormal every week. I once asked the priest how he expected people to believe in these things. He said, "By the time people find their way to me, they don't need convincing."

I figured my father didn't need convincing that the services of a Catholic priest might be useful. Methodist pastors don't do ghosts. I told Dad about the priest and his helpers and asked if I could invite them to drive up from Bayou Pigeon to bless the house. Fine with me, he said. Couldn't hurt.

The night before the priest came, my father lay sleeping in his bed, without his shirt. (August in Louisiana will do that to you.) At one point, he became aware that there were fingers wrapped around his shoulders, and he felt soft flesh on his back. "It was like someone was clinging to me," he said to me at breakfast. "When I realized I wasn't dreaming, I sat up and felt whatever it was let go. I never saw anything, but I heard something that sounded like a pop, and that was that."

"Don't worry," I said to him. "Father's coming."

A couple of hours later, the Reverend Mario S. Termini, a small, gentle man with a wispy white beard and a sparse corona of silver hair, drove up with two older ladies from his church. Shelby Kelly and Florence Delapasse were faithful members of his parish prayer group who helped him in this extraordinary ministry. Shelby, a quiet, broad-shouldered Cajun grandmother, believed she had a special spiritual gift of discernment, which she used in a particular way in cases that involved hauntings and the like. We would soon see it at work.

After briefly greeting my parents, the three sat down in the living room and began to pray the rosary. That done, Shelby asked my mother for permission to walk through the house. All she knew about the situation was that we were having unspecified problems. My mother said yes, and Shelby went straight to my bedroom, where, unknown to her, I'd heard the knocking.

"There's something in that closet," she said. My mother and I began taking things out, looking for any suspicious objects. Shelby turned red, breathed laboriously, and finally, despite the air-conditioning, broke into a sweat.

"I can't stay in here anymore," she said and walked out. I followed her.

She moved into my parents' bedroom and around the end of their bed. As she approached the table on my mom's side, Shelby gripped the bedpost to steady herself and began to shake. Moments later, she stepped up to the table, upon which sat seven or eight framed photographs of family members.

She picked up each one. Most of them she replaced in an instant. Three of them, though, she dropped on the bed as if they had burned her hands.

"Who are the women in these pictures?" she asked.

I looked at them closely. "My grandfather died last week. Those are women who were close to him: his first wife, my grandmother; his mother; and his grandmother."

"Don't you have a picture of him?" Shelby asked.

"Somewhere, yeah, I'm sure."

"Find it. It's important."

Shelby, Florence, and Father Termini returned to the living room and began to pray. A few minutes later, my mother came running out of my bedroom, tears in her eyes, holding a framed photograph of Murphy.

"This was in the closet, behind a board!" she said.

"Give it to Shelby," the priest ordered.

Shelby received it in her lap, put her hands on it, bowed her head, and after a moment or two, whispered something to Father Termini. Father looked at my dad sitting in his chair and said, "It's him, and he can't move on. He needs you to get him forgiveness."

"Tell him, Daddy," I said. "Tell him what happened."

And so my father recounted the family's recent history for the priest. About how he had tried to defend his father from the old man's thieving wife, and how his father had rebuked him. About how he had suffered the wife's scorn patiently rather than dishonor his father. About how that was not the first time in his life that he had done something like that for the sake of his father's love.

When my dad finished, Father Termini asked, "Do you forgive him?"

"Yes."

Father Termini blessed the house, prayed for my grandfather, and scheduled a Mass for two weeks hence, for the repose of Murphy's soul. "You're not going to have any more problems here," the priest said. And they didn't.

But that wasn't the end of the story.

Summer gave way to fall, and then fall to winter. A week before I was scheduled to return to Louisiana for Christmas, my father phoned me in Washington.

"You'll never guess what happened today," he said. "I was in the hardware store, and a town cop comes up to me and says, 'Mr. Dreher, what's the deal with Miss Agnes?' I told him I had no idea, that there was bad blood between us, and we hadn't seen her since we buried Daddy this summer."

"He says, 'Oh, we've seen a lot of her lately. She's been calling us, telling us to send over a car, because doors are opening and closing, somebody's banging on the windows, stuff like that. She called us up the other day in the middle of the afternoon and told us to get over there, because somebody was standing in her front yard throwing something on the ground. We sent an officer over, and she was standing there holding a double handful of butterfly wings, which were all over the yard.'"

"Butterfly wings?" I said to my father. "In December? Where on earth?"

"She's being haunted," my father said. I didn't get the impression that he was all that worried about it. But I wanted to help Agnes if I could. I resolved to go see her over the holidays.

When Agnes opened the door, she was a changed woman. She looked as if she was a hundred years old, as if she hadn't slept in four months. I sat down with her in her living room and asked her to tell me the strange things that had been going on. It was exactly as the cop had told my father, except she added that she could hear a voice above her bed at night. She refused to tell me what the voice said.

I told her what had happened to our family in the week or two after Murphy died and how a Catholic priest had helped us. "Would you like him to come pray with you?" I asked, knowing that Father Termini would likely tell her that she wouldn't know peace until she returned what she had stolen and made things right with my father.

"This is nothing to do with spirits," Agnes insisted angrily. "Somebody's doing this to me by remote control."

"Miss Agnes," I said, "how is that possible? How can somebody make your doors open and shut by remote control?" She wouldn't budge. It was easier for the old lady to believe that what she was living through was a matter of high technology. The preposterous was more credible to her than the paranormal. Getting nowhere, I finally told her good-bye. It was the last time I ever saw her.

Father Termini passed away several years ago, as did his helper Shelby Kelly. I don't know what happened to Florence Delapasse. How I regret not spending more time with them when they were here, talking to them about the things they saw and did when they encountered the supernatural. I'd go see Father Termini about once a year or so, whenever I'd get back to Louisiana. He told me several times that things like what my family went through were common, though people don't like to talk about them. And he often warned me against celebrating Halloween.

"It's the time when Satanists practice human sacrifice, especially of children," he told me when I was in from Washington interviewing him for the first time. "We have satanic cells around here. They exist in all big cities."

I thought he was putting the big-city newspaper reporter on with swamp-voodoo mumbo jumbo, but when I called Sgt. C. P. Wilson, at the time the occult crimes investigator with the Baton Rouge Police Department, he told me that I should believe Father Termini.

"This is difficult to talk about and deal with from a law enforcement standpoint," the police sergeant said to me then. "Some of the stuff is so far-fetched, it's very difficult to convince people that it's really going on."

I don't know what to think about that, and to tell you the truth, I prefer not to think about it. But I tell you this: we don't celebrate Halloween at our house.

It wasn't long before Agnes sold the house and moved into a nursing home. A year or so later, on another visit to Louisiana, I ran into one of her grandsons in the mall. I mentioned the purportedly paranormal activity that I had discussed with her on my last visit.

He laughed and said his grandmother was still experiencing that sort of thing in the nursing home. The way he put it,

I could tell that Agnes's family thought she had lost her mind. Now there was no one to believe her, much less offer her help.

I don't think she was crazy at all. I believe Agnes was being tormented by what she had done to her dead husband and our family. I do not know whether this was my grandfather's spirit, but I do believe that someone was trying to wake her up, to get her to change, to make things right, while there was still time.

Agnes died a few years ago, unrepentant. As far as I know, no one has heard from her since.

Brother John

August Turak

from the Power of Purpose Awards

I feel I can personally guarantee that St. Thomas Aquinas loved God, because for the life of me I cannot help loving St. Thomas.
—Flannery O'Connor

It was 8:00 in the evening on Christmas Eve, and I was waiting for Mass to begin. This was my third Christmas retreat at Mepkin Abbey and my third Christmas Eve Mass.

Mepkin Abbey sits on 3,132 acres shaded by towering mossy oaks. The land runs along the Cooper River just outside Charleston, South Carolina. Once the estate of Henry and Clare Boothe Luce, it is now a sanctuary for thirty or so Trappist monks who live a life of contemplative prayer according to the arduous Rule of St. Benedict.

Already eighteen days into my retreat, I was finally getting used to rising at 3:00 in the morning for Vigils. But this would be a longer day; by the time this special Mass ended, at 10:30 PM, it would be well after our usual bedtime of 8:00 PM.

The church was hushed and dark, and two brothers began lighting the notched candles that lined the walls as the hidden choir's Gregorian chants wafted in from the chapel. This chapel, a favorite meditation spot for the monks, sits just off the main sanctuary.

The magic of these pre-Mass rituals quickly had me feeling as if I were floating just above my seat. Soon I was drifting back to my first service ever at Mepkin, when Brother Robert, catching me completely off guard, urgently whispered from his adjacent stall, "The chapel is open all night!" This man, a chapel denizen who slept barely three hours a night, was apparently so convinced that this was the answer to my most fervent prayer that all I could do was nod knowingly, as if to say, "Thank God!"

The sound of the rain pelting down on the copper roof of the church on this cold December evening drew me from my reveries, and I noticed that I was nervous. Brother Stan had assigned me a reading for Mass, and though I had calmly lectured to large audiences many times, I was, as usual, worried that I would somehow screw up. But reading at Mepkin, especially at Christmas, is such an honor.

I felt that my reading went very well. Upon returning to my seat, I guess I was still excited because, heedless of the breach of etiquette that speaking at Mass implied, I leaned over and asked Brother Boniface for his opinion. Brother Boniface was Mepkin's ninety-one-year-old statesman, barber, baker, and stand-up comic. He managed these responsibilities despite a painful arthritis of the spine that left him doubled over and reduced his walk to an inching shuffle. Swiveling his head on his short bent body in order to make eye contact, Boniface lightly touched my arm with his gnarled fingers and gently whispered through his German accent, "You could've been a little slower . . . and a little louder."

After Mass I noticed that the rain had stopped. I headed for the little Christmas party for monks and guests in the refectory, or dining hall. Mepkin is a monastery of the Cistercian order, whose official name, the Order of Cistercians of the Strict Observance (OCSO), is taken seriously. Casual talking is actively discouraged, and even the vegetarian meals are eaten in strict silence. Parties are decidedly rare and not to be missed.

It was a fine affair consisting of light conversation, mutual Christmas wishes, and various Boniface-baked cookies and cakes, along with apple cider. Mostly I just basked in the glow of congeniality that I had come to associate with Mepkin.

I didn't stay long. It was almost midnight, and after a long day of attending eight church services, packing eggs, mopping floors, feeding logs into the furnace, and helping Father Guerric put up Christmas trees, I was asleep on my feet.

I said my good-byes and headed for my room, several hundred yards away. Halfway to the refectory door I heard the resurgent rain banging on the roof, reminding me that I had forgotten to bring an umbrella. I was cursing and resigning myself to a miserable hike and a wet guest monastic habit for morning services when something outside the door startled me. I squinted into the night and made out a dim figure standing under an umbrella. He was outlined by the rain and glowing in the light from the door. It was Brother John, his slouched sixty-year-old body in a thin monastic habit, ignoring the cold.

"Brother John! What are you doing?"

"I'm here to walk the people who forgot their umbrellas back to their rooms," he replied softly.

He flicked on his flashlight and we wordlessly started off, sharing the umbrella. I was so stunned by his timely offer that I couldn't speak. For in a monastery whose Cistercian motto is "Prayer and work" and where there are no slackers, no one works harder than Brother John. He rises before 3:00 in the morning to make sure coffee is there for everyone and is still working after most of his brethren have retired. Brother John is also what might be termed Mepkin's foreman. After morning Mass the monks without regular positions line up in a room off the church for work assignments, and with several thousand acres of buildings and machinery and a farm with forty thousand chickens, there is plenty to do. (As a daily fixture at the grading house, where I pack and stack eggs thirty dozen to a box, I could easily skip this ritual, but I never do; perhaps it is the way Brother John lights up when I reach the front of the line, touches me ever so lightly on the shoulder, and whispers, "Grading house" that brings me back to it every morning. Perhaps it is the humility I feel when he thanks me as if I were doing him a personal favor.) Yet Brother John keeps it all in his head. Every lightbulb that flickers out is his responsibility. He supervises when possible and delegates where he can, but because he is always shorthanded, he is constantly jumping in at some critical spot. Throughout the monastery, the phones ring incessantly with someone on the line asking, "Is John there?" or "Have you seen John?" And through it all, his Irish good humor and gentleness never fades or even frays.

Now, after just such a day, four hours after his usual bedtime, and forty years into his monastic hitch, here was Brother John, eschewing Boniface's baking, a glass of cider, and a Christmas break in order to walk me back to my room under a shared umbrella.

When we reached the church, I reassured him several times that I could cut through to my room on the other side before he relented. As I opened the door of the church, something made me turn, and I watched his flashlight as he hurried back for another pilgrim until its glow faded into the night. When I reached my room, I guess I wasn't as sleepy as I had thought. I sat on the edge of my bed in the dark for a very long time.

Over the next week I went about my daily routine at Mepkin, but inside I was deeply troubled. I was obsessed with Brother John. On one hand he represented everything I had ever longed for, and on the other all that I had ever feared. I'd read Christian mystics say that God is both terrible and fascinating, and for me Brother John was too.

This had nothing to do with the fact that he was a monk and I was not. On the contrary, Brother John was fascinating to me precisely because I had intuited that to live as he did, to have his quiet peace and effortless love, had nothing to do with being a monk and was available to us all.

But Brother John was also terrible to me because he was a living, breathing witness to my own inadequacies. Like Alkibiades in Plato's *Symposium,* speaking of the effect Socrates had on him, I had only to picture Brother John under his umbrella to feel as if "life is not worth living the way I live it." I was terrified that if I ever did decide to follow the example of Brother John, I would either fail completely or at best be faced with a life of unremitting effort without Brother John's obvious compensations. I imagined dedicating my life to others, to self-transcendence, without ever finding that inner spark of eternity that made Brother John's life the easiest and most natural life I had ever known. Perhaps his peace and effortless love was not available to all, but only to some. Perhaps I just didn't have what it took.

Finally, I asked Father Christian if he could spare a few minutes. Father Christian is Mepkin's feisty eighty-eight-year-old former abbot and my irreplaceable spiritual director. He is slight and lean, with a shaved head and a bushy chest-length beard that he never cuts. Fluent in French and Latin and passable in Greek, he acquired doctorates in philosophy, theology, and canon law as a Franciscan before entering the order at Mepkin. His learning, his direct yet gentle manner, and his obvious personal spirituality make him an exceptional spiritual director. And while he grouses once in a while about the bottomless demand for this direction, I've never known him to turn anyone away.

I told Father Christian of my experience with Brother John, and I told him that it had left me in an unsettled state. I wanted to elaborate, but he interrupted me. "So you noticed, did you? Amazing how many people take something like that for granted in life. John's a saint, you know."

Then, seeming to ignore my predicament, he launched into a story about a Presbyterian minister having a crisis of faith and leaving the ministry. The man was a friend of his, and Christian took his crisis so seriously that he actually left the monastery and traveled to the man's house in order to do what he could. The two men spent countless hours in fruitless theological debate.

Finally, dropping his voice, Christian looked the man steadily in the face and said, "Bob, is everything in your life all right?"

The minister said everything was fine. But the minister's wife called Christian a few days later. She had overheard Christian's question and her husband's answer, and she told Father Christian that the minister was having an affair and was leaving her as well as his ministry.

Christian fairly spat with disgust, "I was wasting my time. Bob's problem was that he couldn't take the contradiction between his preaching and his living. So God gets the boot. Remember this: all philosophical problems are at heart moral problems. It all comes down to how you intend to live your life."

We sat silently for a few minutes while Christian cooled off. Maybe he finally took pity on the guy, or maybe it was something he saw in my face, but when he spoke, the anger in his clear blue eyes had been replaced by a gentle compassion.

"You know, you can call it original sin—you can call it any darn thing you want to, for that matter—but deep down inside, every one of us knows something's twisted. Acknowledging that fact, refusing to run away from it, and deciding to deal with it is the beginning of the only authentic life there is. All evil begins with a lie. The biggest evil comes from the biggest lies, and the biggest lies are the ones we tell ourselves. And we lie to ourselves because we're afraid to take ourselves on."

Getting up from his chair, he went to a file cabinet in the corner of his office and took out a folded piece of paper. He handed it to me and said, "I know how you feel. You're wondering if you have what it takes. Well, God and you both have some work to do, but I'll say this for you: you're doing your best to look things square in the face."

As he walked out the door I opened the paper he had given me. There, neatly typed by his ancient manual typewriter on plain white paper, was my name in all caps followed by these words from Pascal's *Pensées*:

"You would not seek Me if you had not already found Me, and you would not have found Me if I had not first found you."

On close inspection, so much of our indecisiveness concerning life's purpose is little more than a variation on the minister's so-called theological doubts. Ultimately it is fear that holds us back, and we avoid this fear through rationalization. We are afraid that if we ever did commit to emulating the Brother Johns of the world, we would merely end up like the Presbyterian minister: pulled between the poles of how we *are* living and how we *ought* to live and unable to look away. We are afraid that if we ever did venture out, we would find ourselves with the worst of both worlds. On one hand we would learn too much about life to return to our comfortable illusions, and on the other we would learn too much about ourselves to hope for success.

However, in our fear we forget the miraculous.

This fear of the change we need to make in our lives reminds me of an old friend who, though in his thirties and married for some time, was constantly fighting with his wife over her desire to have a baby. Every time he thought of changing into a father, the walls closed in. Fatherhood, he thought, was nothing more than dirty diapers, stacks of bills, sleepless nights, and doting grandparents in every spare bed and couch. Fatherhood meant an end to spontaneous weekends and evenings with the guys. It also meant trading in his sports car for a minivan and a bigger life insurance policy. It was all so overwhelming.

Then one day he gave in. He set his jaw and made the decision to transform himself from a man into a father. He took the chance that he would find himself with all the responsibility of fatherhood and none of its compensations. Then on another day, his wife handed him his newborn boy.

Unexpectedly an inner alchemy began. He melted, and magically the baby gave birth to a father. He was so full of love for this child that he didn't know what to do with himself. While he once feared losing sleep, he now began checking his baby so often that the baby lost sleep. He found himself full of boundless gratitude for his rebirth, regret for the fool he was, and compassion for single friends who simply couldn't understand. He called it a miracle.

Similarly, we must take a chance and act on faith. We must give in, make the commitment, and be willing to pay the price. We must commit to becoming one with that passive spark of divinity longing for actuality that Thornton Wilder, in *Our Town,* describes so well: "Now there are some things we all know but we don't take'm out and look at'm very often. We all know that *something* is eternal. . . . Everybody knows in their bones that *something* is eternal, and that something has to do with human beings. All the greatest people ever lived have been telling us that for five thousand years and yet you'd be surprised how people are always losing hold of it. There's something way down deep that's eternal about every human being . . ."

We must commit to facing our doubts, limitations, and self-contradictions head-on while holding on to this voice of eternity. This eternal voice is urging us to take a chance on an unknown outcome in much the same way that nature's voice urged my friend to take a chance on a new life. And we must fight distraction, futility, rationalization, and fatigue at every step.

From this side of the chasm we may react with dismay at all the work involved in never again "losing hold of it." From this side it may be hard to imagine that just as changing a diaper can be magically transformed from drudgery into an effortless privilege, so can standing outside in the rain for others. But to experience the magic of this transformation, we must put aside our doubts. We must resolve to act decisively while trusting in the aid of something we don't understand and can never predict. We must open ourselves up to the miraculous, to grace.

Working toward this miraculous transformation, rebirth, or inner alchemy is the true purpose of life. This transformation is what the West calls "conversion" and the East "enlightenment," and it is the fruit of our commitment to the authentically purposeful life that Father Christian described so well. It is this transformation that turns work into effortless privilege, makes the unnatural values of Brother John second nature, and proves that the answer to the monk's last prayer each night at Compline for a "restful night and a peaceful death" is eternally ours.

And when we're ready, Brother John will be waiting for us, eager to share his miraculous umbrella. Like him, we will be utterly grateful for who we have become, remorseful for who we were, and compassionate toward those who do not understand.

I am not a monk, but I spend enough time at Mepkin Abbey that Father Feliciano introduced me to a visitor recently and followed it with "He's always here." I am often asked why I go. I go because Brother John loves God so much that he doesn't know what to do with himself. He doesn't know what to do with himself, so he stands outside on a cold Christmas night with an umbrella, waiting. Waiting to offer us some protection and human comfort on our long journey home.

A Spirituality of Aging

Ron Hansen

from *America*

We can be forgiven if we think the spirituality of aging applies only to the septuagenarians among us, but *aging* is a tricky term, for we are aging from the instant of our conception, and then there is the matter of perception: as Victor Hugo noted, "Forty is the old age of youth; fifty is the youth of old age," and as Art Linkletter reported, kids he interviewed recognized only four stages to life: "infancy, childhood, adolescence, and obsolescence."

But generally when we think of aging, we note those years when we become more aware of subtraction than addition, when our minds become slightly fuddled and our bodies shrink or wear down. Gypsy Rose Lee once said, "I've got everything I had twenty years ago—except now it's all lower." We notice the print getting smaller, the stairs getting steeper, sounds getting so muddied that Sprint can forget about dropping that pin; Sprint could drop a ball-peen hammer and we wouldn't hear it.

My mother once passed along the joke that senility has its advantages. For one, you're always meeting new people. Plus, you can hide your own Easter eggs.

Loss and diminishment seem to characterize the later years of many of us. Although the journalist Malcolm Muggeridge claimed, "One of the many pleasures of old age is giving things up," his friend Anthony Powell couldn't agree. "Growing old," the British novelist complained, "is like being increasingly penalized for a crime you haven't committed."

Even in the best of circumstances the elderly in America have become the people of Christ's Beatitudes: those who are poor, those who mourn, those who hunger and thirst for righteousness, even those who are reviled and persecuted. It was Christ's assurance that these are the salt of the earth and the light of the world, but many are skeptical about the real worth of that praise. The losses and limitations that menace the elderly, the slackening of mental powers, the ailments and disabilities that cause their bodies to seem to be their enemies, even the nearness of death—all these degradations can create a realm of terror for the aging, of increasing night and oblivion.

But there is also the promise of a new morning and the possibility for occasions of encounter with mystery, with transcendence, for what the French Jesuit Jean-Pierre de Caussade called "abandonment to divine providence."

"For those who have surrendered themselves completely to God," Caussade wrote, "all they are and do has power. Their lives are sermons. . . . They enjoy supreme bliss because they see the fullness of God's power being exercised in whatever conditions of body or soul they find themselves, in whatever happens to them internally or externally, and in whatever befalls them at each and every moment. Whatever the world offers them is nothing. They judge all things by God's standards."

I find it a nice irony that many Catholic retirement homes today were initially constructed as houses of religious formation, because old age is as much about spiritual formation as the halcyon days of youth are. St. Ignatius Loyola developed a program of formation for those in the Society of Jesus who sought priesthood, a course that included a two-year novitiate of prayer and service experiences and then many years of education in the arts and sciences, philosophy and theology, culminating in ordination. But then, after the Jesuit completed so much hard study, Ignatius required a third year of the novitiate, called tertianship, in which the Jesuit could develop a deeper relationship with God. Ignatius called this period of further spiritual formation the "school of the heart."

We are taught in the school of the heart the crucial differences between acceptance and resignation, hope and dread, doing and being. With faith we can find significance even in the negative aspects of aging, and pride in our increasing contact with that which is the wellspring of our existence. With faith we can find that praying is the one thing we can still do exceedingly well.

When I liken retirement living to religious formation, a school of the heart, I am thinking of it in terms of the story of Jesus, Martha, and Mary in the Gospel according to Luke: "Now as they went on their way, [Jesus] entered a certain village, where a woman named Martha welcomed him into her home. She had a sister named Mary, who sat at the Lord's feet and listened to what he was saying. But Martha was distracted by her many tasks; so she came to him and asked, 'Lord, do you not care that my sister has left me to do all the work by myself? Tell her then to help me.' But the Lord answered her, 'Martha, Martha, you are worried and distracted by many things; there is need of only one thing. Mary has chosen the better part, which will not be taken away from her.'"

We read in the Johannine Gospel that the village was Bethany, that Martha and Mary were the sisters of Lazarus, and that while Jesus was reclining at their supper table, Mary "took a pound of costly perfume made of pure nard, anointed

Jesus' feet, and wiped them with her hair," which parallels the typical preparations of a body for burial in Palestine at that time. We do not know if Luke and John are writing of the same evening, but I like the symmetry: Mary's heeding every-thing that Jesus says and her reluctance to leave his side are forms of adoration and surrender similar to the more ostenta-tious ministrations of anointing Jesus and wiping his feet with her hair. "Mary has chosen the better part," Jesus tells Martha in Luke—meaning do not let diversions, the ordinary distrac-tions of kitchen toil, or even service of others deter you from seeing why you're doing all these worthy things.

It would be wrong to interpret Luke's account as Christ's vote in favor of passivity or retreat from the world—it's quite the opposite. The healthy interiority that is the product of prayer helps us get in touch with our deepest desires, those still-secret needs of our psyches, and helps us explore new areas of learning, seek out wider and deeper friendships, and, most important, serve others as we are still able.

As the French Jesuit theologian and paleontologist Pierre Teilhard de Chardin wrote in *The Divine Milieu*: "If Christ is to take possession of all my life . . . then it is essential that I grow in him not only by means of . . . the supremely unifying amputations of suffering, but also by means of everything that my existence brings with it of positive effort."

Elisabeth Kübler-Ross is justly famous for her studies of the heavenly experiences of those who were judged medically dead but were later resuscitated. The product of her inquiries was her book *On Life after Death,* in which she notes "all the hardships that you face in life, all the trials and tribulations, all the nightmares and all the losses most people view as a curse, as a punishment by God, as something negative. If you would only realize that nothing that comes to you is negative. I mean nothing." Rather, our illnesses, privations, injuries, and misfortunes are opportunities for growth, and each should be accepted, Kübler-Ross writes, "not as a curse, or a punishment, but as a gift to you with a very, very specific purpose."

Annie Dillard was reflecting on that very thing when she wrote in *Pilgrim at Tinker Creek,* "I think that the dying pray at the last not 'please,' but 'thank you,' as a guest thanks his host at the door."

Looking back on our life journeys, we are apt to see many occasions when our grand designs and schemes were impeded or upset, when our hopes and plans seem to have been quashed and our purpose on earth put into question. The hindsight of prayer generally shows us, however, the many ways in which God has helped us revise our headstrong notions, perfected our imperfections, gently guided us onto an unthought-of path, and, as the psalmist puts it, granted success to the work of our hands.

A healthy spirituality of aging will be not just a fond reminiscence of the Holy One's action in our lives; it will include the hope of the future good we can do for ourselves and others, even if only through hospitality and caring. In such a way we will finally graduate from the school of the heart, saying not "please" but "thank you," as a guest thanks his host at the door.

Gaudí, the Blessed

Austen Ivereigh

from *The Tablet*

When, in 1926, God's architect was run over by a No. 30 tram on his way to evening prayer, he was mistaken for a beggar and taken to Barcelona's pauper hospital. His friends found him there the next day. But Antoni Gaudí refused to leave.

"Here is where I belong," he told them.

He had always wanted to leave this world poor, and so he did, two days later, aged seventy-three, honored by a city that universally acknowledged him to be both an artistic genius and a saint.

This is a rare combination. There are no professional architects—let alone musicians, artists, or novelists—in the ranks of the saints. No Mozart or Michelangelo. No Titian. There is only the Blessed Fra Angelico—but he was a friar who painted rather than a painter.

Hence the excitement over the fast-track cause for the beatification—the first stage of the journey to being declared a saint—of one of the great modernist architects of the twentieth century, a scruffy mystic whose most famous work is the awesome, unfinished Sagrada Familia, or Church of the Holy Family, in Barcelona.

The idea of his sainthood was first mooted by an organization officially unconnected to the church, the Association for the Beatification of Antoni Gaudí. It was formed in 1992 by two architects, a biographer, a priest (who has since died), and a Japanese sculptor, Etsuro Sotoo, who converted to Catholicism while working on the Church of the Holy Family. The association began printing prayer cards for private devotion to Gaudí, which are now in ten languages. There are reports of miracle cures, as well as requests for divine favors through the architect's intercession—for the successful completion of an architecture degree, say, or, in the case of a Peruvian priest, for a new church roof.

One of the founders of the association is Josep Maria Tarragona, author of one of the most respected books on Gaudí. As it turned out, "there was much more enthusiasm for the beatification in Rome than in Barcelona," he told me recently at Opus Dei's residence in North London. Before the archdiocese of Barcelona allowed the cause to open in the local church, the pope got wind of the plan. "This Gaudí—is it true he was a layman?" John Paul II asked a Barcelona bishop who was in Rome for an *ad limina* visit. As soon as he was back, the bishop called the association to say he would open the diocesan stage at once. Last year, just eleven years after the association began gathering evidence, a thousand-page dossier was lodged with the Congregation for the Causes of Saints in Rome.

In Barcelona, the opposition has focused not on Gaudí's spiritual credentials—which few dispute—but on the appropriateness of declaring him a saint. José Maria Subirachs, one of the sculptors working on the Sagrada Familia, and an agnostic, argues that Gaudí was a "universal artist" who would be reduced by the church's attempt to canonize him. Gaudí, says Subirachs, was appreciated by people of different religions or none; he belongs to everybody, not just to the church.

But recognizing Gaudí's sanctity in no way threatens the universal appeal of his genius, says Tarragona. Rather, it locates it: the universal values of the gospel and of nature are embedded in the architect's work. "If you know that Gaudí was a Catholic and a mystic, then you have some interpretative keys for understanding his art and appreciating its significance," he tells me. "That doesn't mean a non-Christian cannot understand Gaudí. But you cannot separate the man and his work from his faith."

Opponents of the cause insist, however, that Gaudí's Catholicism is accidental to his genius—even a limitation on it. "They believe that if Gaudí had not been Catholic, he would have been even greater," laughs Tarragona.

The cause for Gaudí's beatification is especially galling to that branch of Catalan nationalism with a secular vision of a free Catalonia. Because nobody doubts the greatness of Gaudí, the nationalists are forced to try to separate him from his deep Catholicism, just as, faced with the Sagrada Familia as the city's icon, they once attempted to turn it into a "temple of culture." Gaudí, a deeply Catholic artist at the heart of the modern Catalan project, "breaks the template" of secularism, says Tarragona. For a pope struggling against the mentality of a Europe unconscious of its Christian origins, that makes a Blessed Gaudí doubly compelling.

Gaudí was recognized from the beginning as a genius, the extraordinariness of whose work lay in his attempt to harness the forms of nature. From a childhood spent contemplating nature's forms, he observed that the abstract geometry of human architecture was foreign to nature, which instead had forms that were fibrous—wood, bone, muscle—and shapes formed by gravity. Forms in nature, he saw, served a function.

If an architect looked for that function in his work, he could arrive at beauty, whereas if he sought beauty, he would reach only art theory, or some abstraction. Gaudí's major works—La Pedrera, Güell Park, and not least Sagrada Familia—are initially upsetting, because they are more like nature than architecture. For the same reason they are both captivating and timeless. Everything in his work, Gaudí would later say, "comes from the Great Book of Nature"; his task was that of "collaboration with the Creator."

Gaudí never bothered to attend classes for his architecture degree, but his commissions spoke for themselves. He fast became the city's best architect—and its most expensive. In his twenties Gaudí was a wealthy dandy, dressing extravagantly and giving orders to his workmen without getting down from his horse-drawn carriage. Like Picasso and Dalí after him, Gaudí "was conscious of his brilliance," says Tarragona. "He knew that Western architecture had come so far, and [that] he was way ahead of it."

This was a recipe for endless egotism and future burnout. But he was knocked off course by the refusal of the beautiful and wealthy Pepita Moreu to marry him. Another woman to whom he proposed shortly afterward broke off the engagement to become a nun.

Almost no one questions the sincerity or depth of Gaudí's conversion at the age of about thirty-one to a life of austerity and prayer. The turnaround was gradual—Tarragona describes it as a "nine-year process"—but was no less dramatic for that. Thereafter, he remained alone, caring for the two surviving members of his family—his father and his orphan niece—until they, too, died.

The turning point came in 1883, when he took over the plans for the Sagrada Familia, which would become the grand synthesis of his life's work. (The church is still unfinished, but now that it is being visited by two million tourists a year paying eight euros each, finance is no longer a problem, and work is proceeding fast.) He had by then come into contact with two key figures in his conversion: Juan Bautista Grau, the bishop of Astorga; and Enric d'Ossó, who was later declared a saint. Gaudí began to shed his wealth and to adopt the life of a pauper and mystic. Every day for the rest of his life he read the Bible, attended Mass, said the rosary, and confessed under the guidance of his Oratorian spiritual director. He seldom traveled, wrote little (although he was a great talker), and read selectively: by his bedside was *L'Année liturgique* by the abbot of Solesmes, Dom Guéranger.

His asceticism could be extreme: people recall him nibbling on pieces of bread or eating lettuce leaves dipped in milk. One Lent, in 1894, he had to be ordered to eat by his spiritual director after a radical fast left him at death's door. But his asceticism was mostly directed at his work, which he approached with characteristic obsessiveness and self-sacrifice. "Life is love, and love is sacrifice" was one of the architect's bon mots. "Sacrifice is the only really fruitful thing." The idea is embodied in his great church, which he conceived as an "expiation" for the sins of the world.

But it would be wrong to portray Gaudí—as some writers clumsily do—as a "hermit." For his doctorate in journalism Tarragona has collected all the Barcelona newspaper and journal articles that featured Gaudí in his lifetime—about three thousand, an average of two a week in his supposedly "hermit" years. "He was talked of a lot and was a recognizable figure about town," says Tarragona. "If you look at all the newspapers of the period—Catholic, traditionalist, Republican, Masonic, anticlerical—without exception, they speak of him with absolute reverence."

Gaudí was active, for example, in a Catholic group of artists, the Cercle Artístic de Sant Lluc, headed by Bishop Torras i Bages; he also belonged to the League of Our Lady of Montserrat, a Catholic nationalist group that advocated a pluralistic, democratic Catalonia (as opposed to the Integrists or Carlists, who spurned both Madrid and Rome). His nationalist credentials are impeccable: Gaudí, who always spoke Catalan, was arrested under the dictatorship of Primo de Rivera (1923–30) for refusing to speak Castilian.

A craftsman by training, Gaudí was demanding of his workers but also endlessly kind. In his lifetime the Sagrada Familia was some way from the city center, in one of the city's poorest barrios, where he was loved and respected. In 1909, during the so-called Tragic Week, when a third of the religious buildings in the city were torched by anticlerical mobs, the Sagrada Familia was spared. When the next spate of church burning happened after his death, in 1936, the tombs at the church were desecrated—except for Gaudí's.

The architect's struggle against his natural inclinations— especially his bad temper—was titanic. "God has given me the grace to see things with absolute clarity at that moment," he told a friend. "I have to say things just as they are, without beating around the bush, and of course people are annoyed." But it is asked of saints only that they struggle, not necessarily that they succeed. "I am a fighter by nature," he confided to his spiritual director the day before his accident. "I have always fought, and I have always succeeded, except in one thing: in the struggle against my bad temper. This I have not been able to overcome."

He came to exhibit to a heroic degree, says Tarragona, the virtues, both theological—faith, hope, and charity—and cardinal: prudence, righteousness, strength, and temperance. The Carmelite Sisters of St. Joseph who used to clean his room were told by their founder, Mother Rosa Ojeda i Creus, that they should take their spiritual cues from Gaudí. "We who have taken a vow of poverty must learn much from him," she used to say.

Accustomed to the Romantic icon of the artist as tortured and alienated, people find it hard to grasp that Gaudí could be at the same time mercurial and deeply prayerful. Interestingly, the idea of the suffering artist is strong, too, in Gaudí; however, it is the suffering not of alienation but of a loving response to God. He used to say that the joy of artistic creation was so immense that if the artist did not respond through fasting, suffering, and poverty, he would be in some way *descompensado*, "overcompensated."

But even if his personal holiness is not in dispute, what role do his works play in the cause for his beatification? If the Sagrada Familia is evidence of Gaudí's holiness, why does not the Sistine Chapel make Michelangelo a saint?

Tarragona believes that while plenty of artists have been touched by divine inspiration in their work, few—"perhaps only Bach, but of course he wasn't Catholic"—have exhibited the intimate relationship with God that is proper to a saint. "Mozart could write the Coronation Mass without having a devout life," says Tarragona. "God gave him the grace, as of course he did with Michelangelo in the creation of the *Pietà* or the Sistine Chapel. But in Gaudí we get both divine inspiration and a personal life proper to a mystic."

Gaudí, in short, was a lay professional who became holy in response to divine artistic inspiration—which is why part of his cause must be his work. Because he had total creative freedom in the last years of his life, his works are inseparable from his holiness, says Tarragona, in the same way that the sanctity of St. John of the Cross, for example, cannot be considered in isolation from *The Spiritual Canticle* or *The Dark Night of the Soul*.

One of the signs of the congruence of his creativity and his holiness was that Gaudí's greatness increased with age, unlike that of other artists—Mozart, say—who either burned out or died young. Like Bach, Gaudí worked every day of every week. After the Sagrada Familia commission, his life became for the next forty years ever more geared to God. So much so, in fact, that when people pointed out that the church would never be finished in his lifetime, Gaudí would just shrug.

"My client," he would say, "is not in a hurry."

God Gave Me a Gay Son

Thomas A. Nelson

from *Notre Dame Magazine*

Mark gazed out the small window of his dorm room. It was a Saturday morning, and the bitter bleakness outside matched his mood. He may have made a mistake going to school so far north and so far from home, but he had chosen this school in northern Michigan because he loved the natural environment of the northern country, where he could ski, hike in the woods, and enjoy the serenity of this sparsely populated place. Mark had also thought college would bring people into his life who wanted a good educational experience, people with whom he could be open and find companionship.

But the dream turned into a nightmare.

The source of his anguish—the realization that he was attracted to some of the young men around him and the conviction that those feelings would disgust people—fed his terrible feeling of isolation and left him feeling numb. He didn't think he had done something wrong; he wondered if God had made him that way. But it wasn't a problem he could talk about, not to family, not to friends. No one could help him. Even God didn't answer.

So on this Saturday morning Mark realized that nothing really mattered anymore. His situation could only get worse. And while it frightened him—having considered it for quite a long time—he also knew how he could fix it. The only way to confront this demon was to end it all. Nobody would understand anyway. *He* didn't understand. But he knew he was gay, and he knew being gay was an abomination. So he would put an end to his agony. Committing suicide, he decided, would be less painful to his family than revealing to them who he really was.

Mark sat down at the small table at the end of his bed. He picked up his pen and wrote:

The fog thickens . . .
I try to see through it at my paper and pen.
Through them to the world.
The fog thickens . . .
They pound and laugh all around me,
Their laughter a testimony to my despair.
"All that you need is wine and good company."
I can be like them,
I am not alone.
I can be like them,
I will find happiness.

I cannot be like them,
I am alone.
Why not just rest and forget about it?
Rest and forget about it.
Outside the wind howls.
Inside the silence howls.
It has been snowing for some time now,

And my soul is buried in a drift.
The wind blows too hard for the plows to clear the roads.
I am destined to die in a snowdrift.

Then Mark went to the window and looked out at the gray blur of the winter storm. He thought: *It will be easy. Just take that bottle of prescription painkillers. No more anguish. No more self-hatred. No more struggling. The hell with it then. God forgive me.*

And the thought became the act.

The pills went down easily, and he lay down on the bed to die.

It was a sunny afternoon in San Francisco. My wife, Trish, and I had just arrived at our room in the Mark Hopkins Hotel for a business conference. It had been a long and tiring trip from Michigan.

"Tom, look," Trish said. "These flowers are from Tracey."

She was holding a mixed bouquet sent by our daughter, with a card that read: "Welcome to San Francisco. Call me when we can get together. Love, Tracey."

My wife sighed as she collapsed into the plush leather chair. "Aren't our kids wonderful?"

"They sure are," I replied. "I guess we're pretty lucky."

As I gazed out the window, savoring sights I hadn't seen in thirty years, I thought how lucky we really were. Our six children all seemed so perfect. The company was paying our travel expenses, and tonight we were going to have dinner with Tracey. We hadn't seen her in over a year. Her older sister was back home at work, and the rest of the kids, including our son, Mark, were safely away in college. My life was going pretty much according to the script I thought I had authored.

Raised in a traditional Catholic family during the 1930s and
'40s, I enjoyed a thoroughly Catholic education, from elemen-
tary school through college. The church was a central part of
my loving family. My two brothers and I were expected to
excel in everything, but our grades in religion classes got
special scrutiny.

After graduating from Notre Dame, I had certitude about
religion and morality. My understanding of the contemporary
culture was defined by a black-and-white perspective on most
issues. I felt comfortable expressing my views on those things
and often did. I was solidly Roman Catholic, more than proud
of it, and ready to defend it to anyone. My parents seemed
reasonably satisfied with the product of their labors: we had
survived the Depression and the Second World War, and we
children were all healthy and college educated. It was the
'50s, and I was a young man ready for career, marriage, and
family.

Trish came to our marriage as cloaked in traditional
Catholicism as I did. She, too, had enjoyed sixteen years of
Catholic education, though she wasn't the cocksure moralist I
was. As was typical of that time, our children came early and
often. Having five girls and one boy in the first eight years
of marriage was part of our education. We felt blessed with
such healthy children, and I often bragged about how we were
"growing up with our kids." We faced the usual hurdles that all
families experience, and we handled them as best we could.

Soon the children were entering their teen years, the
church was adjusting to Vatican II, women were being liber-
ated, the United States was at war in Vietnam, and the moon
was the latest frontier for human progress. Hippies were in
vogue, a president was assassinated, and immorality seemed
rampant. Just about everything that appeared certain was
being assailed. The world was going to hell and outer space at
the same time.

Despite our best efforts, Trish and I couldn't totally shelter our family from the dangers and challenges of those days. However, armed with self-assurance and the absolute truth endowed to us by our Catholic background, we confronted each issue with confidence. We sought opportunities to promote family discussions, and our dinner hours evolved into a ritual of stimulating conversation. We would discuss any topic that any family member wanted to explore.

I indulged in a lot of preaching during those family sessions. Often, I simply pronounced the official church teaching as the final word on an issue. I cautioned my children to beware of all the false propaganda bombarding them from virtually every source. When they were confronted with a difficult choice, I urged them to consider the right thing to do. I would stress: "Use your intellect. Decide for yourself. What does the data say?" I wanted these as family mottoes. Of course, Vatican II challenged some of my long-held convictions. Still, my immutable Catholic dogma continued to fortify my comfort. In hindsight, I realize I was suffering from an intellectual coma. My brain was in hibernation.

Eventually, at a few of these dinnertime discussions, the subject of homosexuality was ever so timidly broached. "What do *you* think, Dad?"

I don't remember who asked the question, but it wouldn't have been Mark. It had to be one of the girls. They liked to challenge "Dad's agenda." While I would have preferred to avoid discussing anything relating to sexuality, my answer was fairly easy, and it came quickly. I knew the words of the magisterium: "An abomination." "Sex is reserved for marriage." "Love the sinner; hate the sin." "Natural law." And so on. Concluding with a short lecture on the virtue of chastity, I clearly conveyed "End of discussion . . . next topic."

It was a well-intentioned automatic response, but one that made open dialogue of a difficult topic impossible. Little did I realize the struggle my son was undergoing at the time. My pontificating was stifling his attempts to communicate and secretly causing him to question the worth of his very existence.

As Trish and I were taking a stroll in San Francisco two days after we arrived, she gently posed a question that was to greatly influence my life. "I've been worrying about Mark," she said. "He's been seeing a lot of one young man and hasn't been dating girls. The thought of it scares me. Does it scare you?"

My initial reaction was a quick little laugh. Then, a bit sarcastically, I said, "Relax. There's nothing to worry about." But a wave of panic swept through me. *My God! No. It couldn't be.* The seeds of doubt took root. Dreading the prospect, I resolved to confront my son as soon as we returned.

Mark defied all the popular stereotypes I believed about what being gay meant. I was sure I could recognize a gay person from a mile off. But my son was just too masculine. He never displayed the effeminate traits that I was certain a homosexual male would exhibit.

I recalled as typical of his "masculine toughness" an incident when he was about eight years old. He was to play in an important junior hockey game, but he had a dental appointment to have five teeth pulled on the same day. His mother insisted that the hockey game was second priority. So, after a little nitrous oxide, the five teeth were extracted. After this ordeal, Mark proceeded to the restroom, where he promptly vomited. Then he calmly returned to his mother and said, "Now can I please go to the hockey game?" She took him, and he played. This was my homosexual child? No way.

Nothing during Mark's childhood gave any sign that he might be gay. There was none of the verbal violence that many young gay people endure from earliest childhood—no jeering, no "faggot" or "queer" talk. He was seemingly happy, well-adjusted, and "straight."

Of course, there was that time in high school. Late in the afternoon one pleasant spring day, Trish and I received a phone call from Mark's after-school employer. Mark had not shown up for work. His employer said he was concerned because "Mark is never late. He's my most reliable employee." We didn't know where he might be, and a series of frantic telephone calls availed us nothing.

Eventually, we discovered that our son had withdrawn all his savings from the bank, and he and two friends had taken a bus to Florida. While he soon telephoned to assure us of his safety, he had apparently resolved not to return. We were dumbfounded. Fortunately, economics intervened. When his money had nearly run out, Mark was relieved to learn that we would not only welcome him back, but we were ready to wire him the return plane fare as well.

This incident was definitely disturbing to us, so we decided Mark needed professional counseling. The counselor came highly recommended and with all the appropriate credentials. His evaluation quickly assured us that Mark's Florida escapade was little more than a "lark—a healthy, youthful rebellion." His prompt conclusion: "Your son is a very normal, well-adjusted, and intelligent young person. It would be a waste of your money and my time to proceed any further." Without hesitation, my wife and I accepted his reassurance and breathed a sigh of relief.

Like most parents, Trish and I had hopes and dreams for each of our children. These entailed the usual trappings of a happy, fulfilled life: health, education, spiritual welfare, material success. However, again as most parents do, we unwittingly tried to fit our children into preconceived molds. Now, older and perhaps a little wiser, I marvel when I observe how different each of my adult children is. They are like startling reflections of the incomprehensible diversity of God's creation. Nevertheless, back then, I certainly had some definite assumptions about my son's future. The possibility of having a gay son was not part of my plan.

Homosexuality was a dim and distant issue about which I knew and cared little. It has been said that possession of absolute truth is the end of learning. While I understood that there were many things I didn't know, moral issues were not among them. I knew the rules, and I knew the reasons.

What I did not know then is that the suicide rate for young gay people is *three times* that for other teens. Their struggle to accept their sexuality is too often a lonely battle devoid of family support, not unlike my son's. I fear that too many parents suffer, as I did, from rigid moral convictions. Unfortunately, the result can be the ultimate of tragedies—the loss of a child.

Mark overcame his act of utmost despair only through courage and God's amazing grace. Years later, when I learned of his suicide attempt, Mark told me that as he had waited for death to release him, he went through what he could only describe as a unique religious experience in which God spoke to him in a special way. Somehow he abruptly realized that God had created him just as he was, and so there must be some good reason for being who he was. God surely accepted him as he had created him, and Mark should do likewise. He ran to the bathroom and forced himself to vomit the painkillers he had taken. Had he reacted soon enough? The next thirty-six hours proved to be a benumbed and desperate struggle as he dragged through a drugged twilight, not daring to allow himself any sleep for fear that there would be no morning.

My son did survive his trauma. Mine was still to come.

My wife and I had returned from San Francisco. I was with Mark, who was coming home for his semester break. We were alone in the car. Freeway traffic was light, and I decided it was time to take the plunge. There was no prologue, no warning. I was abrupt and blunt.

"Mark, are you gay?"

He looked startled. After a long pause, he quietly said, "I don't want to talk about it."

I thought for a moment and said, "I guess you've just answered my question."

To which he responded, again very quietly, "I guess so."

With those three little words, my world came crashing down on me. Despite my mental preparation for this moment, I was speechless. We were almost home, and neither of us spoke another word for the rest of the trip. I was still in shock when we walked into the house. My wife looked at me and knew instantly that I had asked the question—and what the answer had been.

My son's disclosure was a personal trauma. Initially, I didn't think about the implications for him. My immediate reaction was mostly self-focused. "What have I done wrong? What will family and friends think? Can he change? What should I do? What *can* I do?" I alternated between heartache, anger, and fear. This son of mine, who had once seemed so perfect, was now a torment. Of course I loved him still. But how could *my* son be gay? He wasn't like *that*. It simply wasn't plausible. I had to fix it. Yet what could I do?

I realize today how little I knew. My understanding of homosexuality encompassed little more than a now-defunct

Freudian theory that a homosexual child is the result of a weak father and a domineering mother. In my selfishness, it gave me some immediate solace to place the blame for this tragedy on my wife. *Of course—it's her fault. A dominant woman!* I thought. But I quickly found this strategy neither right nor helpful. It simply added stress to our marriage. Still, there was this *weak father* thing. I just couldn't accept that idea. Maybe there *was* something I could do. I realized I needed more information.

I began by reading every book or article on the subject of homosexuality available in the Detroit libraries. I had an insatiable need to learn everything I could. Gradually the myths began to dissolve. I learned that some 5 to 10 percent of the population is estimated to be homosexual. Homosexuality is probably not the result of environmental conditions but more likely genetic. It is the professional consensus that it cannot be changed and that attempts to do so can be distinctly harmful. The best minds in the fields of medicine, psychiatry, psychology, and biology generally agree that homosexuality is a normal variant of the human condition and certainly not some disorder that requires treatment. Even during that period, without the Internet, there was plenty of "data" showing that homosexuality was a normal condition.

Following this phase of my education, I began to realize that this issue was about my son and not so much about me. My spell of self-indulgence was fairly brief, but I still feel sad that I wasn't more help to Mark, immediately and without equivocation. He needed it. He deserved it. My intellect began to awaken from its hibernation. I felt more empathy, something I had felt too rarely in my past. My expectations for the conventional gave way to a frightening vision of my son's future. What was he going to face? It was not pleasant to contemplate.

All too often the gay community faces the risks of violence, discrimination, harassment, and ostracism. The chances of my son being accepted as a normal member of society seemed to be slim to none. Otherwise decent people often oppose, with self-righteous, moralistic railing, some of the most fundamental human rights for gays—rights that the rest of us take for granted.

Homosexuality is not a condition I would have chosen for my son. So why not celebrate the gift of a gay son?

Since Mark's disclosure some twenty years ago, I have come to know many gay people. We have dined together, walked together, traveled together, worshiped together, and laughed and cried together. I have some new stereotypes as a result. Almost without exception, I have found my gay friends to be likable, lovable people of high integrity. And more than that, most seem to have a resilience, a forbearance for life's burdens. I have been deeply moved by their tales of adversity overcome. I have seen them subjected to insults and abuse by their government, their churches, their neighbors, and some even by their families, and then seen them respond with a patience I envy. They have taught me how quiet tenacity can achieve success in the face of the most discouraging odds. I have watched gay people, young and old, routinely living lives of often heroic charity toward others, done without fanfare. It is a charity most of us professing Christians would find difficult to match, and it is too often accomplished while deprived of the nurture of "organized" religious groups that seem focused only on condemning them. By their example, they have shown me how to truly love my neighbor.

These experiences forced me to confront the fallacy of my former arrogant certitude. I realized that I had been given the opportunity to learn from everyone I meet in life but that I had been passing up many potential professors. I resolved to attend all my classes in the future. Through my involvement in a group called PFLAG (Parents, Family, and Friends of Lesbians and Gays), I have come to know many other parents of gay children. I have learned about the anguish and abuse that society irrationally inflicts on their families. It has been a journey to a new perspective that has enabled me to better understand my own failings and the world around me. My struggle to be more fair-minded and less judgmental has been made easier.

I also have watched my children gain a unique appreciation of others. And I've found that not having all the answers has given me a closer, more trusting relationship with my God. It has been a bonus to watch Mark mature into the successful, happy adult he is today.

Yes, Mark does experience more than the normal challenges of our culture that straight folks endure—despite the fact that being gay is only one small part of who he is. Yet he now seems to shrug off most of those burdens. He prefers to think of them as society's problems, not his. His attempt to lead a normal and happy life has been largely successful, but that other reality is always lurking in the background.

There is one challenge that gives me, his father, much anguish. It is his feeling of utter rejection by the Catholic Church. After his long struggle to find a place in it, it seems that too many official proclamations only remind him that he is considered depraved, disordered, and intrinsically evil. He has given up on it. I am at a loss to convince him otherwise. I've discovered that when I apply my newfound empathy, I have a tough time not reacting as he has. I can only continue to pray and wonder about what it all means. I try not to let it destroy my own love for the church. Sometimes I'm not too successful at it.

I know that many of my Christian fellows and others would take grave issue with some of my views. They would argue with sincerity the same positions I once so adamantly held. I am well aware of the popular biblical arguments that are used to condemn homosexuality. I am also glad that some of the best biblical scholars have given us new insight into those literal interpretations touted by many to support their castigation of homosexuality. Sadly, too, I regret the promiscuous immorality displayed by some in the gay community. Yet I doubt that any segment of our society has a monopoly on immorality; heterosexuals are certainly just as accomplished at this. I also share a deep concern for the welfare of what some describe as the "endangered" American family, but heterosexuals have done their share to break up marriages and threaten the health of the American family. And how can we justify dishonestly labeling as "special rights" those basic civil, legal, and human rights the rest of us take for granted?

Much of our Christian rhetoric is anything but Christian. I have personally seen the tragic human consequences of intransigent, righteous moralizing. I nearly destroyed my own son with such "loving" dogmatic proclamations.

Now, late in my journey, I find myself with more questions than I had when I started. Answers that I once was so sure of have fallen far short. Some have proved to be false. I have found many answers in unlikely places and from unlikely people. Most of the answers have given me joy; a few have made me sad. Many of my unanswered questions my beloved church will not even address, acting as if the "data" were irrelevant. Like me, the church has feet of clay. I realize now that absolute truth is a far-off goal, attainable only in the hereafter. Perhaps now, though, I have a better understanding of humanity's common struggle. For a Christian, I think, the task is to try to comprehend and apply the truth and the full implications of Christ's final plea: "Love one another as I have loved you."

For me, discovering the complex meaning of this message has been a long journey that continues to this day. It has been a difficult lesson for me, and one that might never have happened. But, fortunately, God gave me a gay son.

Yes, God gave me a gay son—a fact I celebrate today—a son who has had a most profound effect on my life. While it was obviously not his intention, Mark, just being who he is, has taught me more about myself and about the nature of the Creator—his unfathomable love, and the diversity of his creation—than perhaps all the academic and social experiences of my past. I believe most parents would agree that they learn from their children, probably as much as they teach. I have certainly enjoyed this reward of parenting from all six of my children. Being the unique individuals they are, they have all taught me—in their own special way. But Mark had the advantage of being gay.

The Eyes of the Icon

Sophie Masson

from *Image*

*In these films [*Signs *and* We Were Soldiers*], but especially in a new movie, a monumentally risky project called* The Passion, *which he co-wrote and is currently directing in and around Rome, [Mel] Gibson appears increasingly driven to express a theology only hinted at in his previous work. That theology is a strain of Catholicism rooted in the dictates of a sixteenth-century papal council and nurtured by a splinter group of conspiracy-minded Catholics, mystics, monarchists, and disaffected conservatives— including a seminary dropout and rabble-rousing theologist who also happens to be Mel Gibson's father. . . . Perhaps nothing Gibson has done will serve as a more public announcement of his faith and worldview than the project he's now completing in Rome. The* Passion *is a graphic depiction of the last twelve hours in the life of Jesus Christ, based on biblical accounts and the writings of two mystic nuns. Gibson is returning to the director's chair for the first time since* Braveheart *in 1995, but he will not appear on screen. There will not, in fact, be any big stars. Nor will there be subtitles, which might prove a challenge for many moviegoers, since the actors will speak only Aramaic and Latin. Gibson has said that he*

hopes to depict Christ's ordeal using "filmic storytelling" techniques
that will make the understanding of dialogue unnecessary.
—Christopher Noxon, "Is the Pope Catholic . . . Enough?" The
New York Times Magazine, *March 9, 2003*

Three icons hung on my parents' bedroom walls when I was
a child in Sydney, Australia. Two were Russian, one Greek.
The Greek one was my favorite. It depicted St. George and
the dragon, the painting on the wood overlaid by a sheet of
beaten, carved silver metal, so that George was clothed in
armor and the dragon in shining scales. Saints' stories, in
general, didn't attract me; a romantic, thrill-seeking, dreamy
child, I vastly preferred stories of knights and ladies, wizards
and fairies. I found many of the saints either dull or weird,
but St. George, as represented on the icon, was different. He
could be tied to the stories I loved: Arthur fighting monsters
or Perseus slaying the Gorgon. This icon appealed to my
father, too, though my mother thought it overdone, veering
dangerously close to the fantasy she rejected.

The Russian icons were different. Looking at George
might conjure up thrilling or frightening images of battle, of
clashing sword on scale and fiery breath (and what about the
horse, I always wondered—how did he escape being frizzled
alive? Did George's holiness magically protect him, too?), but
looking at the other icons was uncomfortable and haunting.
Both had been painted by an exiled Russian artist my father
had come to know, a man who suffered greatly from the loss
of his homeland and had rendered the icons in the brooding,
uncompromisingly intimate yet stylized Byzantine-influenced
Eastern Orthodox manner. One was of a pensive Virgin Mary,
her cheek against that of her infant child; the other was of
Jesus as a man. Highly emotional depictions, they were also
restrained. Mary's hair was hidden under her veil; her great
dark eyes and those of her thin child rested just beyond us, as

if she were contemplating what must happen to her beloved son. The manhood portrait showed a dark-eyed, wavy-haired, plainly dressed Jesus, both man and Christ: we were told it showed him just before his trial, torture, and death.

Every Palm Sunday, my father would drape a blessed palm frond over the icon of Jesus, where it would stay, quietly drying out, till the next Palm Sunday. This icon's eyes prickled under my skin and made me scurry quickly out of the room if ever I was sent there on an errand. Those eyes spoke. They were alive, they looked deep into you, and their gaze followed you around the room and out of it. As a child, I could not identify the expression that lay in those eyes, though I knew it was neither joy nor anything cheerful. All I knew was that I wanted to get away from their scrutiny. Later, I could see suffering there, yet also a charismatic certainty. The sorrow in Mary's eyes was mixed with loving pride, but the sorrow in Jesus' was mixed with a certainty of mission. This was passion: the fire of inner conviction despite dreadful ordeals. And religion to me lived in that expression.

Sometimes, if one of us children was suspected of telling a lie, my father would take that child by the hand, stand him or her in front of the icon of Jesus, and say, "There. Now, look at him and repeat what you said." He could not believe that anyone could stare into those eyes and tell a lie. My mother, more cynical, would watch you carefully, able to detect (mysteriously, it seemed to me then) whether you were telling the truth. As a miracle-believing child, I found it hard indeed to lie while looking in those eyes; in the arrogance of adolescence, I turned away. Even so, it was hard not to flinch, for those eyes seemed to know already that you were going to persist in your lie, and to look at you not angrily, or even with judgment, but with that inner, fiery courage, that sorrow, and also the endless knowledge of just what humans were capable of.

Everyone over the centuries who has ever thought about him has had a personal image of Jesus the man: reformer or zealot, lord or rebel, epitome of love or fierce warrior, mystic or clear-eyed storyteller, heretic or defender of tradition. None of these alone tells the whole story, of course; each one tells us more about individual and cultural temperaments than about the Son of Man. Over the centuries, the church has attempted to equalize the portrayal of Jesus, to meld his complexities into a full portrait. Not all of these attempts have succeeded; the danger is of making him either bland or contradictory. Besides, the experience of Christianity is not just institutional but deeply personal and intimate. It is inevitable that one's picture of Jesus will be colored by one's experience and temperament, and for me, that started very early in childhood. Part of what haunted me about the icon was that I knew it also represented my father's religion, dominated by a seeking, questioning intelligence and a fierce passion. My parents' bookshelves were lined with books on all aspects of religion, especially heresies. Heretics are those who both question and seek certainty, whose passionate attachment to their own emotional truths leads them into conflict.

My father, a fervent, mystical Catholic, has also always been interested in the fringe, the esoteric—in short, the heretical. Not for him the calm of jogging along with the mainstream church; restlessly curious, fearful that hope was in fact hopeless, he constantly sought assurance, even if of a negative kind. On his desk, in a velvet-lined box, rested an ancient crucifix on which an ivory Jesus hung. Nothing startling about that, except that the suffering man's arms were pointing almost directly upward in a narrow embrace. It was a Jansenist crucifix, demonstrating through gesture the notion that only a small proportion of people would be saved. A keen awareness of evil and suffering haunted my father, whose childhood had been both privileged and tormented. He could talk about the human capacity to inflict pain only in frighteningly passionate terms; the war and accompanying family trauma had shattered his childhood and made him, in a sense, an exile. It predisposed him to fear that he was a heretic at heart, and yet to glory in that. For him, the stories that resonated most clearly were of hopeless causes, of fierce courage and resolution crushed by a greater power.

For a long time he was interested in that rather narrow version of Christianity, the religion of the Cathari. As both a southern Frenchman and an emotional seeker, he was moved to tears by their story, which he spent hours studying years before it became fashionable. Their central tenet—that the world was the creation of the devil, not God; that all of us were exiled spirits yearning for our true home in heaven; that our flesh only imprisoned us in evil and fear—resonated with him. (Incidentally, it has always seemed strange to me that New Agers and others are attracted to Catharism, with its uncompromising rejection of our world. Perhaps they imagine that Catharism is about vague, airy-fairy, feel-good thoughts, a precursor to their own beliefs that was crushed by a wicked Catholic establishment.)

The crusade against the Cathari led to scenes of utmost brutality and cruelty, where hideous things were done in the name of God—by the Cathari as well as the crusaders, incidentally, despite modern perceptions. It developed into a bloody and protracted civil war, from which wealthy Occitania emerged beggared and humbled. It led, too, to the building of aerie-like castles on the edges of abysses, to standing resentments and long memories.

Including the long memory of my father. In my mind is a picture of an impossibly long, steep path up a bleak peak that rises Golgotha-like above a fold of green hills. I am the only one walking up with my father; my mother and the younger children have stayed below. Dad walks quickly, his face taut with the things he has read about, the hideous things that happened here at Montségur, the Cathari's last stronghold. Here, in meadows that stretch under the ancient crag, 211 men, women, and children were burned to death.

Later, people will travel from all over the globe to see this place. But for now, interest in Catharism is a fringe thing, a harkening back to a regional, religious past that no one rational or modern wants to know about. My father and I reach the top of the crag. The old fortress stands serenely in the wind, gutted, its walls almost intact. The beauty of its surroundings sits oddly with our knowledge that it is a graveyard. Dad stands in the citadel silently, and I walk amid the broken stones and earthen floors, all the fury of the crusaders left of this once impregnable place. The people who lived here, who held out so desperately, were offered mercy if only they would convert back to Catholicism, but, stiff-necked, the majority refused and marched to their fiery deaths with terrifying pride.

I was moved by this place, by the sorrowful and fearful knowledge that people would choose death over life. I loved life myself—for me the world was beautiful and rich and filled with hope and thrill, suffused with loving Presence—but I still unconsciously understood how such a death was possible. Because I knew that for my father, it was real. He could see himself being led out to the stake, or fighting to the death. For him, the thought of death validates life; the grand rejection of compromise is what moves him. There is contempt in his voice when he talks of the Protestant French king Henry IV blithely giving up his religion to become a Catholic, famously explaining that "Paris is worth a mass" (although, paradoxically, my father also has admiration for the king's peasant pragmatism and cunning).

The Cathari—grand, doomed, misreading the temper of their times—were romantic figures for my father, particularly when study of them was a fringe interest. Later he came to disdain them, after Emmanuel Le Roy Ladurie's famous *Montaillou: The Promised Land of Error* brought them to hundreds of thousands of people, awakening postmodern interest in their doctrines and way of life. Now that Catharism has become, as has regionalism, a respectable study and hobbyhorse, he rejects it.

My mother never had much patience for the Cathari; more orthodox and less emotional in her Catholicism than my father, she is also more suspicious of the romantic rejection of compromise. The romantic and the grand often led to hideous excesses: wasn't that one of the lessons of history? She argued with him over the Cathari's doctrine, with its inflexible and unpleasant rejection of the earth and the body, and over his fear that the world was only a place of evil and suffering. For her, the eyes of the icon were painted eyes, an expression in paint of the artist's faith. She shared the artist's faith, if not his Russian Orthodoxy; she loved the painting as a work of art, but she set no store on the power of the icon itself. The romantic outlook would demand that a glimpse into those eyes set off instant, permanently transforming remorse; in her realism, she suspected that such a reaction might lack staying power.

She did not trust my obvious emotion in the face of those eyes. She saw my reaction as real, but real in the way that the tremors of feeling induced by ceremony, magnificent music, or beautiful words are real: the feelings exist, yet perhaps they are not enough to sustain a faith. That was my problem, she said. In the presence of beauty, I felt the breath of God, just as I did when contemplating the world—for in my fortunate childhood, surrounded by love and possessed of a hopeful nature, I saw a benevolent world, though I knew that malevolence was real. Spiritual presence for me was completely real, as it is now; I felt it in every pore of my skin and every inch of the air around me. The world was the creation of God, I knew instinctively, and could not be that of the devil, whose wish was to destroy the world and tear out the very roots of heaven in his rage and sorrow. Yes, I knew God was there—but I could not describe God to my parents. I knew they wanted passionately to impart to me their own images and perceptions. I knew they wanted me to reflect them back to them, but I couldn't. Something prevented me from explaining. It is perhaps part of the reason I took so to reading and writing; I wanted to escape into a world where there was no need to explain, to proclaim, where Presence was unspoken but utterly real, and manifest in a whole range of ways.

The image of Jesus in the Bible filled me with admiration and wariness in equal measure. My siblings and I knew the Gospels well (and were even introduced to some of the Apocrypha), and indeed I read the entire Bible as a child. Attuned to story, I loved the Old Testament particularly, but I also loved Jesus' parables, and the narrative of his passion moved me greatly. The idea that he was the Son of Man and the Son of God, God made flesh, said to me that we human beings were microcosms—within our own bodies and souls—of the Presence in the world. My differences with my parents were not over questions of whether God was real or whether Jesus could be both divine as well as human. There were other things involved. For on another level, I was also afraid of that charismatic certainty, that wild passion, that fierce intelligence and contradictory wisdom so characteristic of the man we glimpse in the Gospels. I retreated from his uncompromising nature, from his terrible knowledge of suffering, of hopeless causes, of inhumanity—and from the heaviness that it all entailed, the gravity beside which the thistledown-light, merry, and melancholy things I loved might be brushed aside and destroyed. Did Jesus ever laugh; did he ever do anything for the sheer fun of it? I could not remember one instance of it in all my readings, though I remembered moments when he was depicted as enjoying food, drink, and friendship. The eyes of the icon did not let me dream. They pinned me to the wall.

It was inevitable that, individually and together, my parents should reach a decision that marginalized them still further, in religious terms. The changes brought about by Vatican II hurt them deeply, though for a time they tried to live with them. It was not just the abandonment of the beloved Latin Mass and what they saw as the banalization of ritual, but what they saw as a radical change of heart in the church. They felt the church had betrayed them and itself and had, in an attempt at staving off secular hostility, caved in to a world that sought its destruction. The shock of this betrayal hit them each in different ways. My mother felt abandoned by the church hierarchy; my father, less respectful of authority, was furious that they would dare change, unilaterally and without consultation with their own congregations, what he deeply valued—that strong sense of sacrifice, suffering, and transformation at the heart of the old words of the Mass.

For a time, my parents tried to discuss this directly with the hierarchy, sending densely argued and sometimes arrogant letters to bishops and priests. To my horror, they also challenged religious teachers at our schools, both laypeople and nuns. To no avail. They were told in sometimes blistering terms to be quiet and accept, that if they were true Catholics they must submit to papal decisions no matter what they thought or felt. One or two of the clergy even made the mistake of calling my father a heretic, a charge he both expected and feared. The choice of word seemed calculated to inspire fear; a threat of persecution, of excommunication, hung heavy in the air. It has been the unfortunate tendency of some in the church to deal with heretics by confronting them head-on, without indulgence, understanding, or even psychologically wise tactics, and for people like my father, this inevitably feeds a sense of persecution that is not altogether paranoid. To be fair to the recipients of my parents'—particularly my father's—challenges, Dad's attitude was "take no prisoners." Compromise was utterly rejected, the charge of heresy was turned back on the mainstream church, and the result was foreseen.

So one Sunday, instead of walking up to our local church as usual, we drove some distance to a most unromantic, most unatmospheric community hall where a Latin Mass was being celebrated. On the way home, my parents discussed the whole thing excitedly, as if new heart had been put into them, while, in the back, I felt my heart sink. This declaration of defiance boded ill for us children, who wanted to be like everyone else. At our Catholic school we were already known to the nuns as the children of the heretics who had rejected the pope's rulings. We wanted to be part of seventies culture, but we were forced back into an ancient past by our stiff-necked parents. No one else we knew at school or in the neighborhood went to Latin Mass. Driving through the suburbs on Sundays, we children sometimes felt like prisoners in a time capsule, travelers from another planet. The passions of faith were cool in most people we knew, for in Australia religion has fallen on rather stony ground, but in the Latin Mass Society, which grew out of such community Masses, they burned white-hot.

The Latin Mass Society was made up of a heterogeneous collection of people whose only common links were their fierce passion for their religion, their determination to defend it, and their certainty that while others might call them heretics, they were preserving the truth. Mavericks all, contrarian and individualistic, they were natural rebels—but rebels defending tradition. They came from all walks of life, all ethnic origins, all spiritual bents: warriors and mystics, gentle souls and conspiracy theorists, aesthetes and those of simple tastes, excited types and ironic jokers. The priest who led this community of odd rebels was a man both quiet and fierce, whose dreamy eyes focused sharply during the Mass and whose overwhelming experience of Jesus was expressed utterly in the Latin words. The mosaic of character and life story made Latin Mass Society meetings, held every month after Mass, rather filmic, even surreal. As cruel teenagers whose greatest fear was being uncool, we siblings lampooned them in private, but now I am moved and amazed by the human variety: a family dogged by tragedy, whose faith never seemed to waver despite the most hideous trials; a young railway man with an old face and a wonderful combination of laconic Irish wit and Australian disdain for jumped-up authority, who told marvelous stories of the follies of railway bureaucracy with a perfectly straight face; a round, humorous captain of the merchant navy whose earthy jokes made some less-robust members look a little panicked; a father of a large family who published romantic novels under a female pseudonym; a slight, still-eyed lady who had experienced visions of the Virgin Mary, often in the most unpromising circumstances; two men named Geoff and Jeff who always came together; a kind Lebanese lady who called everyone "Love," wore hats shaped like pie plates, and sang enthusiastically in a shrill voice (and whose niece later became a modestly famous world music star); and the tribe of Gibsons, led by fiercely intelligent, confrontational, red-headed Hutton and his calm, quiet, smiling wife, Anne.

There was more than your usual quotient of martyr material in those diverse characters. Each had sacrificed something to come there, from dearly held notions of papal infallibility to a more convenient Mass time at the church up the road. Many had wrestled with their consciences and with habits of obedience. And in a gathering such as this, you could at unnerving moments see incarnated the human yearning for

certainty in the divine, a certainty some are willing to die—
or even kill—for. I do not mean by this that any of the society's members would have hurt anyone, or hurt themselves;
mostly they lived lives that were very much the same as other
people's. I mean that in this one aspect of their lives, they
had made their choice and were certain of it. Their assurance
enabled them to withstand immense pressures and to apply
pressure in return. Very little was spared in the fight between
the church hierarchy and the Latin Mass rebels; both religious
and social allegations—of heresy, subversion, immorality, and
general sinfulness—were leveled at both sides, in a dirty war
indeed. It was not a simple black-and-white matter, either,
though one was always enjoined to take sides; for someone
like me, always attempting to keep a balance, to mediate, to
compromise, it became unbearably difficult. My childhood
ended up both vaccinating me against religious extremism and
making me painfully aware that religion was a real, important,
emotional truth that wouldn't just go away because secularists
wished it to.

My father, who at work juggled figures constantly, despite
a professed hatred for math, became the treasurer of the
Latin Mass Society, and Hutton Gibson became its secretary.
Hutton and my father were of a similar passionate temperament, which meant they sometimes agreed and sometimes
argued bitterly. Both were larger-than-life figures whose
complicated characters dominated their families. Both were
well-read, fiercely opinionated, endlessly curious, yet also
tyrannical at times; it wasn't easy for either of them to give
ground to anyone else—and if you didn't give, you were
crushed. Certainly being a member of the Masson family
has schooled me in the art of dogged resistance, honed my
analytic skills, and taught me to defend my position with fire
and spirit. It was the lukewarm who exercised and annoyed

my father; what was the good of arguing with someone who'd rather give ground than fight?

The late Anne Gibson and my own mother were both calming influences on their emotional husbands, and the gaggles of Gibson and Masson children followed along willy-nilly, whether willingly or not. We were pressed into practical service, too—setting out chairs and flower arrangements, carrying in paintings, and so on—because the church met in a borrowed community hall. One of the Gibson girls, with red hair that fell to her waist and an angelic soprano voice, sometimes sang at High Mass, along with the more usual male choir. I didn't know what she or any of her siblings felt, deep down, about their parents' religious fervor, and didn't ask; after all, I knew only a little more about my own siblings' feelings. As young people brought together only by this one thing, we and the Gibsons and other Latin Mass families circled warily around one another. My younger siblings played occasionally with the youngest Gibson boy, and my sister Camille and I cast many furtive glances at the older boys, with their long hair and swaggering walks, and particularly one, a quietly observant and handsome young man with piercing blue eyes and fair hair touched with gold. But it was the adults who argued and discussed and shared their religious passions; the young people were in the background, mostly tongue-tied in front of their formidable and feisty parents.

By this time, I was in my mid- to late teens, filled with fire myself but of a different sort, made up of romantic passion and the thrill of creation, for I was writing, writing, writing. In that strange space that is the home of creativity, that for me is full of a glorious freedom, joy, love, and ecstasy, I knew why I had been born. I felt close to God in a way that I still could not explain to my father, who would have labeled me a pagan, or a pantheist. (Being called a heretic does not predispose you to sympathize with heretics of a different bent.) I pretended to be cold to my parents' religious passion and kept my own feelings secret; I did not want my parents labeling them or trying to change them. I gripped my loved things tightly—my books, stories, music, and poetry, and all the myriad sensual manifestations of the world—and sullenly, doggedly resisted any assault on my citadel. By that age, I had also discovered the myths, legends, literature, and art of the Celtic peoples, whose worldview chimed so well with my own that finding it felt like discovering the key to the meaning of the world. (The graceful combination of immanence and transcendence that is expressed so powerfully and naturally in Celtic poetry and art shows perhaps why the Celtic peoples so readily accepted Christianity, without the martyrdom and persecution that had attended its introduction into the Roman world.)

Jesus was still an important figure to me, but by this time I had rebelled completely against my father's interpretation of his life. This was the seventies, and the most resonant image of Jesus for many young people was of the gentle, bighearted rebel. On Good Friday, the day in the year most dominated by Jesus' suffering, we fasted and went to an emotional Mass where just before 3:00 PM the priest would call out the last words of our Lord: "My God, my God, why have you abandoned me?" And then he would whisper, "Into your hands I commend my spirit." After that came the evocation of Jesus' death. No matter how often I'd heard it, this moment always sent shivers up my spine: the combination of wild revolt and fear, followed by that astonishing acceptance. How he had suffered! What courage he had! How could I ever measure up to such things?

But back home, I drew rebellious pictures of a bearded, long-haired, bright-eyed young man who bore a marked resemblance to the Gibson boy my sister and I most admired: handsome, quiet, long-haired Mel. I would look at the dark, difficult Jesus of the icon and think, *I don't want to die early just for some cause. You don't have anything to say to me.* I would refashion my image of the Messiah; I would reject my father's religion; I would question all its irksome restrictions. Why should I, because I was female, have to cover my head in Latin Mass? Why should God extend his blessing to only a small section of the population? Why did faith always mean you had to be prepared to fight, if not to the death, then certainly to a standstill? Fighting against the papacy held no interest for me at all; the sometimes bizarre conspiracy theories aired by some of the society's members made me prickle with embarrassment. I irked my parents with questions, with challenges, but most of all with a mask of carefully cultivated indifference that I knew would hurt them the most. It was the only way I could protect myself from the passion that burned so hotly in them.

Still, the eyes of the icon haunted me. They would not let me go, and over the years they continued to force me into more and more uncomfortable examinations. It's more than spiritual ecstasy you need, they challenged me; it's not just knowing naturally that God is there, that Presence is real. It's not just a question of reflecting wonder and beauty and meaning; it's not just within the benevolent that you will find Presence. It's also there in human suffering and rage. What does it mean to be the savior of the human race? What does it really entail? As a child, I'd been taught that original sin was not sexual, not about covering yourself up when you were naked, but about recognizing the evil that lay in every human heart, that capacity for choosing between God and the devil that had birthed human consciousness and made us what we were: exiles from Eden eternally searching for peace, yet so great that God had chosen to incarnate his Presence in one of us, who reached out to all of us, to the kingdom of God within each one of us. Swimming naturally, unconsciously, in the ocean of mystery and wonder, yet riven deep inside by our own complex nature, many of us refused to see further than our own navels, and was it any wonder? Was it any wonder that some of us chose to cast the Presence away and either blandly ignore it or deliberately, proudly choose its negation, the adversary? No, it was no wonder.

As I grew older, these things became more and more important, the lessons of experience and observation merging in me with a visionary temperament to strengthen, to blood what otherwise might have been a frustratingly evanescent, bloodless gift of expression.

As a secretive, imaginative child, speechless before my parents' religious passion, I had thought it a hindrance, an obstacle to my own vision, but also something embarrassing, because it was unspeakable. Today, the understanding of that passion burns deeply in me; I am still able to feel what religion actually is for those who fight for it, and in its name. Unlike many of my siblings, including my sister Camille, who became a painter, her art expressing her religious feelings—and unlike Mel Gibson, too—I do not share my parents' religious practices. I have held fast to my childhood apprehension of the Presence in the world. I have chosen to cast my own understanding of the world and human nature through the medium of fantasy, which is suffused with spiritual presence, though it does not often mention God by name. His Presence is instead implied by metaphor and allegory and symbol, the language that resonates most deeply with me. In our days, it is in fantasy, both in literature and film, that we get the clearest, most daring, and yet most traditional explorations of the sacred and the spiritual. Through this immensely popular medium, all kinds of ancient ideas are being broached and explored once again, but in an allusive, elliptical way that feels natural to me.

I have never forgotten the eyes of the icon. I do not think anymore that they forbade me to dream, or condemned me, though my original perception still remains. I know now that the eyes expressed many things, and I still haven't gotten to the bottom of them. But George and his dragon were also necessary, and not inferior, either. Both my art and my spiritual perception have been strengthened and deepened by the kind of childhood I had. This strange, thrilling, frightening, confused time we live in is my time, and I am not afraid of what others think anymore, or of whether I am breaking a taboo: the taboo that says that religious passion must not be written of, or, if it is, that it must be either condemned or ignored, and certainly not expressed by artists who want to be seen as relevant. The times have shown us that this taboo blinkers us to reality. We need the exploration of religious passion in all kinds of ways. Perhaps for another member of my Latin Mass congregation who became a practicing artist, Mel Gibson, some similar personal and artistic trajectory began at the East Lindfield Community Hall, leading him into the most difficult exploration of them all, the direct filmic depiction of Christ's passion.

I Hear Confessions

Kevin M. Tortorelli

from *National Catholic Reporter*

I hear confessions at St. Francis of Assisi Church in midtown Manhattan. It is possibly my chief work. The two confessionals are spare, small, and often cold. In summer, awful odors can linger, a composite perfume, cologne, or spent breath. The stale smell of a cigarette occasionally rises from clothing or is borne on the spoken word. My tiny fan does battle with it. This is the setting in which a variety of people go to confession. They are at all points on the journey to God.

Some are in the midst of an anxiety attack and desperately want to be at peace. Delicately, I try to deepen self-understanding, but their defenses can be formidable: fear of change, emotional withdrawal. I encourage them to have a spirit of openness and to maintain a network of good friends. I urge them to live a balanced life: to eat well, pray, be productive, keep up with family and friends, get some exercise. I think perhaps these words may give birth to insight that will liberate them from fear and set them in the right direction.

Many people are dealing with anger over genuine hurts and over their inability to forgive someone. Perhaps bitterness and resentment have killed off a valued and cherished relationship. We both sense that the way forward lies in forgiveness. But how does it work? I offer the thought that forgiveness breaks a chain to old hurts and their hold on me. It frees me from reacting to what has been. I am increasingly free to choose how I will respond and live. That at least is my own experience of forgiving another. It is a little morsel to offer, but with it God can feed them.

Some have suffered abuse. They visibly struggle to speak about a consuming darkness. The voice may crack: "Where was God when I needed him?" I wonder the same thing. They have decided they will forgive God. I am stung by their greatness of heart. The next person has knocked down one or another of the commandments as if it were a bowling pin. There is no boasting. It was a slipup. But sometimes there is sadness in the voice. Something is a besetting sin. Will he ever be free of it? I wonder how to encourage him. I urge him to be patient with himself and with God's grace, to live each day simply and roundly, to appreciate that maturity and self-control take shape over time. I emphasize the strengths he has already developed. He listens and shares a smile.

People say they have failed to trust God. A man in his fifties is let go after a quarter century with his firm. A single mother is knocked back into welfare. A grandmother discovers that her grandson, a teenager, has dropped out of school or is running with the wrong crowd. A breadwinner is taken seriously ill. At home there is a disabled child. The outpouring numbs me. I am pained that my comfort and security threaten to distance me from them. Do I even know what it means to be tempted against trusting God? When did *I* last pray, "Lord, save me?"

I hear, as a chorus at my center, the words *O man of little faith* . . .

Though small as the mustard seed, faith knows a good, hearty laugh. Take the little boy who confessed adultery.

"And what is that?"

"When you hit your sister."

We talked about getting along with, even loving, one's sister. That proved too much for him. Defeated, I told him, "Next time, just tell the priest you hit your sister." With that agreeable conclusion, he was out the door.

Then there was the little boy who didn't know how to begin. Trying to jolt his memory, I asked when his last confession was. In an instant he was on his feet. Throwing open the curtain, he yelled into the crowded church, "Ma, when was my last confession?"

Mortified, she lowered her head. I went out to her, steeped in apologies. She was gracious, and at the telling of the tale we shared a soft laugh together.

People's faith is gentle and humble. In particular, the poor pray with profound gratitude for all God's blessings. I think to myself, *What blessings?* But I learn from them. They are my teachers. And then there are intimate moments. Sobbing accompanies words of sorrow. Absolving, the Spirit lifts us into the kingdom of the beloved Son and strengthens us to walk as children of the light. At the end, a pause, a breath of silence before God, who has moved among his children: *Go in peace.*

The Secret

James Martin, SJ

from *Portland Magazine*

Five years ago this summer I knelt on a cold marble floor in a church in Boston, before a Jesuit archbishop. Placing his hands on my head, he prayed silently. By tradition, when I stood up I was a priest.

The ordination Mass is one of the most elaborate liturgical ceremonies in the Roman Catholic Church, with rituals stretching back to the earliest days of Christianity. At various points in the liturgy, one hears echoes from the worlds of both late antiquity and the Middle Ages. Near the beginning of the ceremony, those to be ordained, the ordinandi, kneel before the bishop and place their hands between his, recalling the pledges of fealty offered by vassals to their lords. ("Do you promise respect and obedience to me and my successors?" asks the bishop.) After declaring their obedience, the men lie prostrate on the bare floor, facing the altar, their hands tucked under their foreheads, in a gesture of humility before God and the church. Following the episcopal "laying on of hands," the ordinandi, clad in white albs tied with cinctures (a traditional symbol of chastity), are vested with the symbols of the priesthood: the long stole (a sign of authority in ancient Rome) and the chasuble (the poncho-like garment of Greco-Roman times). Finally, they are anointed on the palms of their outstretched hands with the chrism, or holy oil, as the bishop pronounces a ritual formula: "May Jesus preserve you to sanctify the Christian people and to offer sacrifice to God."

In light of the sexual abuse crisis in the Catholic Church, the above paragraph carries overtones that are both unwanted and unavoidable. Today the "obedience" of priests and bishops to the church suggests a desire to protect an institution at all costs. "Humility" before the church may connote a willingness to overlook crimes committed against children. Any "authority" that priests enjoy, at least in this country, has been severely eroded. The notion that a cleric would be needed to "sanctify" others may seem an arrogant one, effectively elevating the priest from the plan of the average layperson. Indeed, that ordination is limited to men is a continuing source of pain for many Catholic women (and men) and underscores the insular nature of the hierarchy, a target of withering criticism during the last two years. The term "laying on of hands" after the sexual abuse of so many minors is especially fraught. And chastity may be the last thing associated with the contemporary Catholic priesthood.

But this collision of the new and the old, the contrast between beautiful ideals and sometimes ugly realities, as well as the negotiation of clerical life during a period of crisis are only a few of the hurdles that face the Catholic priest today.

Though the life of a priest is almost unimaginably rich, many people I meet are interested not in the joys of celebrating Mass, the deeply moving experience of hearing confessions, the challenges of balancing the active and contemplative lives, or the struggles of representing a church in a secular world, but in something else: the sexual life of a priest. Such interest only intensified in the wake of the clerical abuse crisis, which led many Americans to conclude that priests were (pick one): sexually active, utterly unaware of their sexuality, pedophiles, or, in general, wholly incapable of keeping their promise of celibacy.

Even strangers and the most casual of acquaintances have felt free to ask me questions about the following topics: my sexual history (before and after my ordination), my sexual orientation (and that of my brother Jesuits), and even whether I think masturbation violates the vow of chastity. It is as if the mere appearance of a Roman collar sets people free from the normal conventions of contemporary conversation.

One challenge, therefore, is not to take personally even the most offensive comments, and to bear in mind that many such questions come from a lack of knowledge about the priesthood. After all, there are fewer and fewer priests around. A recent Georgetown University study reports that the number of Catholic priests in the United States declined from roughly 59,000 in 1975 to 47,000 in 2003. The number of active priests (the total figure includes retired clerics) is pegged at only 22,000. While the Catholic population in this country has grown rapidly (from 49 million in 1975 to 63 million in 2003), the number of priests has declined dramatically. So it is not surprising that misunderstandings would grow over time.

Underneath some of these pointed and personal questions seems to rest a natural curiosity about the meaning of sexuality, which the Catholic Church has defined as a precious, indeed holy, gift not to be squandered. Whatever one may think about the church's attitude toward sex, this facet of Catholic moral theology always strikes me as healthier than almost any other message that one receives in a culture in which sex and sexuality are increasingly commodified.

Such questions about sexuality are neither surprising nor difficult to understand, especially these days. During the early months of the sexual abuse crisis, in 2002, as I learned more about the grotesque crimes of the former Boston priest John Geoghan, I found myself repulsed by the details of his actions and outraged that such a person would have been allowed to continue functioning as a priest. Still, I remained hopeful that such cases would prove rare.

But as more and more instances of abuse were unearthed, and evidence uncovered that some bishops had moved abusive clerics from one parish to another, I found myself confronting, as did most priests, a host of warring emotions. Certainly I knew that many bishops had in the past relied heavily on the expertise of mental-health professionals, who had sometimes given even serial abusers clean bills of health. Nonetheless, the consistent reshuffling of abusive priests time and again flew in the face of basic common sense. Eventually, I found myself angry (at the ineptitude of many bishops), embarrassed (as the term "pedophile priest" slowly entered the lexicon), sorrowful (over the awful plight of the victims), confused (at the bewildering variety of reasons offered for the scandal), and despairing (as the litany of cases seemed without end).

As the crisis wore on, every priest seemed to admit to one tipping point—the piece of news that finally moved him, if even temporarily, to a state of demoralization, depression, or despair. Perhaps it was reading the repellent details of a predatory priest's crimes in one's diocese; perhaps it was meeting face-to-face with a victim of abuse living in one's parish; perhaps it was knowing a colleague who was abruptly removed from active ministry as a result of a decades-old crime. For me it came as I read the nearly unbelievable story of Paul Shanley, the serial abuser and former member of NAMBLA (the organization that celebrated "man-boy love") who was called "a priest in good standing" with "no problem that would be a concern in your diocese" in a letter from Cardinal Bernard Law's office to the bishop of San Bernardino, California. For a while I wondered how I could publicly represent a church that countenanced or at least tolerated criminal behavior. And for the first time in my short career as a priest, I was embarrassed to wear the collar.

The fallout from the crisis in the lives of active priests—that is, the vast majority, who have led healthy lives of service—is immense. Beyond disappointment in the institutional church and sorrow for the victims of abuse, there are less well-known consequences for priests: tightened budgets resulting from justifiably large legal payouts means less money for educational and social-service programs in parishes; working with lay-run organizations like Voice of the Faithful, as well as developing and implementing sexual misconduct policies, rightly demands more time and attention; dealing with bishops whose schedules are now packed with meetings with lawyers and psychologists means that other pastoral issues must take a backseat.

There are other, more personal, results. Many priests will now, as a rule, never get close to a child, no matter how benign the circumstances. After a recent Sunday Mass, a young girl standing beside her mother spontaneously hugged me, and I was surprised to find myself wanting to push her away. I wondered: Will this hug be later misinterpreted? Priests and members of religious orders teaching in Catholic schools say that their work has been affected dramatically. One friend who works in a Catholic high school for poor boys is frequently approached by students seeking counseling about their complicated family lives. In the past, the students could count on privacy. Now they must air their problems in a classroom with an open door and so are less willing to discuss their struggles, for fear of other boys overhearing. While these concerns are a small price to pay for the crimes committed by priests, they nonetheless have an effect on many hardworking priests who struggle to carry out their day-to-day ministries.

Why do I stay in a church so clearly flawed? Why do I stay a priest? These are fair questions, and they remind me of Father Andrew Greeley's trenchant comment that the question today is not why so many Catholics leave the church, but why they stay.

First reason: I freely made a vow to God, and I intend to keep my word.

Second reason: I love being a priest. I feel it is where I am meant to be. I love celebrating Mass, presiding at baptisms and weddings, preaching homilies, hearing confessions. I love talking with strangers on the bus or subway about faith and doubt. The Trappist monk Thomas Merton expressed this gracefully when he wrote, around the time of his ordination in 1949, that the priesthood was "the one great secret for which I had been born."

Third reason: As anyone who reads church history, I am not surprised by the presence of scandal and even grave sin in the church. As any organization, the church has long had its share of fools and villains, some of whom have held high offices. After all, St. Peter, by tradition the first pope, sinned famously, denying Jesus three times before the Crucifixion. Centuries later, Renaissance popes like Alexander VI (of the rapacious Borgia family) and Paul III were widely known to have granted ecclesiastical offices to their illegitimate children and grandchildren.

Even the greatest of Christian saints recognized this. During the fourteenth century, when two and sometimes three men claimed the papacy for themselves, Catherine of Siena excoriated members of the hierarchy for their corruption. "You are flowers that shed no perfume," she wrote to a group of Roman cardinals, "but a stench that makes the whole world reek." (When asked how she could judge this from so far away, Catherine replied that she could smell the stink in Siena.)

While historical precedent does not excuse the contemporary sins of abusive priests or the bishops who reassigned them, it stands as a reminder, especially to Catholics accustomed to thinking otherwise, that the institutional church is made up of sinful human beings and is therefore constantly in need of change and reform: *Ecclesia semper reformanda.* The theological model of the church as a "pilgrim people," always on a journey, was underlined by the Second Vatican Council in its 1964 *Dogmatic Constitution on the Church,* a key document of the reforming council: "The Church . . . at once holy and always in need of purification, follows constantly the path of penance and renewal."

But it is insufficient simply to admit sinfulness. As any priest worth his salt will tell you in the confessional, a penitent also needs to show a "firm purpose of amendment" and a desire to undergo a form of penance. There is also the long-standing requirement to participate in the larger reform of the community. During the Donatist controversy in the fourth century, when a group of Christians wanted to admit only the "holy" into the church, St. Augustine disagreed, arguing that the Christian community should welcome as well those who have sinned and repented. Yet as Peter Brown notes in his biography *Augustine of Hippo,* the saint understood that this was only part of the solution. Early Christians striving for holiness must, of necessity, coexist with other sinners in the church, but they should also "be prepared, actively, to rebuke and correct them."

I see some signs that after a very public "rebuke," penance and reconciliation are finally beginning in the Catholic Church in the United States. Last July, the new archbishop of Boston, Sean Patrick O'Malley, a Capuchin Franciscan, declared on the day of his appointment his desire to work for reconciliation, no matter the cost. "People's lives are more important than money," he said simply. O'Malley's subsequent swift resolution of legal settlements, his willingness to sell the archbishop's palatial residence in Brighton, and his personal outreach to victims of clerical abuse show that it is possible to work for reconciliation with compassion, intelligence, and, yes, speed. The 2004 report from the National Review Board, which showed that 90 percent of all dioceses were now compliant with the "Charter for the Protection of Children and Young People" implemented by the U.S. Conference of Catholic Bishops, was also a generally positive sign.

At the beginning of the ordination Mass, the bishop offers a short homily to the ordinandi. Though the rubrics of the ceremony provide a standard homily, the bishop has the option of forgoing this in favor of a more personal message. But I'm always a bit disappointed when he chooses to do so, since the traditional text includes this exhortation:

"Let the example of your life attract the followers of Christ, so that by words and actions you may build up the house which is God's church."

All in all, that's a good goal for priests during this period of crisis, and I look forward over the next few years to helping rebuild a church sorely in need of repair.

Our Lady of Sorrows

Michael Mack

from *America*

Why my mother chopped off her hair, followed me to the
        school bus stop
that morning in second grade,
I didn't know. Or why

she bent down sobbing
Don't let go of my hand.
How long did we stand by the 7-11?
Other kids hushed, watching.

When the bus clunked to a stop
I climbed on last, grabbed a seat in back.
My mother outside, hand curled on my window,
her face a blur

as the bus jerked away.
The kid beside me punched my arm:
Who was that man with you
crying so hard?

I said I didn't know.
Three times I swore I *don't know him.*

A Brief War Primer

James V. Schall, SJ

from TCRnews.com

Since and because of the murders of September 11, 2001, this country and other nations have been at war. For many people, it is difficult to form a clear idea of what it is all about. In most wars, the enemy side is a nation-state. This war seems at first to be a different kind of war, and it is.

But it is still a war.

It might be of some use to spell out, as a matter of opinion, the main elements of what this war is about. The most dangerous position is the one that does not know that a war exists, and that we are its main target because, evidently, we are the only power willing or able to stop the enemy, in his own estimation, from achieving his end.

1. This is a real war with an active, dangerous enemy. It is at its heart a civilizational war, however reluctant we might be to acknowledge it. It is not due merely to a few "fanatics," not forgetting that the few have always led great movements.

2. The enemy is not directly a nation-state, but that does not mean it is not dangerous or capable of highly damaging activity. It does use nation-states who will cooperate with its

goals. Had all ten or twelve planes that were evidently planned to be used on September 11 reached their targets—probably the White House, the U.S. Congress, the Supreme Court, the Sears Tower in Chicago, perhaps the Golden Gate Bridge or George Washington Bridge, and other similar targets, not only American—this country would have been much more seriously paralyzed than it momentarily was. The order to ground all planes on September 11 was little short of brilliant.

3. Recently, al-Qaeda planners have been surveying American financial institutions and power grids. This plotting suggests that the enemy is shrewd and knows how to inflict maximum damage at the heart of a modern, complex society. It is probable that the enemy has or will have some nuclear weaponry that need not be delivered from the sky. Nothing indicates that this enemy will not use such weapons when it can. If it is not physically stopped, it will use them.

4. Above all, this is not a war against "terrorists." This definition of the enemy has been most unfortunate. It has obscured the face of an enemy that must be seen and dealt with. The word *terrorist* makes it sound as if those who attack us are members of a political-science subset that appears out of some oft-recurring aberration throughout the globe. It abstracts this enemy from the cause that actually motivates it. Terrorists, supposedly, can be "explained" in terms of just reaction to maldistribution of goods, or poverty, or by some social justice excuse. Little or none of this sort of explanation applies here. The enemy is not motivated by these reasons.

5. The war has been caused, planned, and carried out by specific religious groups within Islam. They claim, and probably justly, according to their own lights, to be implementing the demands of their religion. They have a pious long-range purpose: to destroy the opponents of Allah and to make everyone else a believer. Generally speaking, we are so indoctrinated with ecumenism or liberalism that we

cannot comprehend how this thinking could be credible, even though, historically, the expansion and consolidation of Islam were largely the result of such successful military forces. Islam did not, except in rare cases like Indonesia, expand by "peaceful" means. It expanded by war and military control, particularly against, but not only against, Christian peoples.

6. Not all Muslims follow these groups, but many, probably the majority, are sympathetic with their goals, especially when they seem victorious. From within Islam, it is almost impossible to oppose these movements except by Muslim government forces, who are themselves often under threat from these same movements if they do not support them.

7. This war is not "caused" by Israel. Obviously, Israel provides grounds or pretext for complaint. No one, even itself, holds that Israel has done everything right. But if Israel were to disappear tomorrow, the same problem would exist, probably on a greater scale. Israel may well be the most visible example of what our cities and countrysides would be like if similar militant Muslim forces began operating effectively with similar tactics within our borders or in those areas in Europe where Muslim populations are steadily increasing.

8. This is not a war of American imperialism caused by a misreading of the doctrine of Woodrow Wilson about making the world safe for democracy. Everyone in the West, including the president and the pope, would like to see a "democratic" government in Islamic countries, where there are at best only one or two. The basic pattern of Islamic government is a military overlord elevated to some monarchal status and usually in control of the army. Recently, Afghanistan and Iran, and some others, have seen more specifically religious leaders take over rule.

9. Almost nowhere within Islamic states is there anything like freedom of religion. What is meant by *tolerance* is merely second-class citizenship as opposed to elimination. There are

no "conversions" except to Islam permitted. All non-Muslim religions are placed under legal constraint, when not subject to violence. There has been a constant flow of Christian martyrs within Muslim states in the last half century, Sudan being the most notorious. Christians within Muslim lands have largely fled to the West when they could.

10. The purpose of this war, from the American side, is very straightforward: to seek out, identify, and destroy those al-Qaeda and other militant Muslim forces that have initiated the war and continue to carry it out. There is no "dialoguing" with these forces. They have a mission and intend to carry it out. The only thing that will stop them is force. No argument, dialogue, or pressure will be effective against them. The failure to understand the nature of this implacable enemy is itself a cause of its continued success.

11. Can we lose this war? It is quite possible, particularly if we fail to see that it is a war of civilization in the eyes of those who attack us. The Spanish election was a case in point. The blowing up a train just before an election was enough to panic the Spanish electorate to vote for the weakest possible opponent. In all probability, this was al-Qaeda's strategy for the American elections. The fact that Bush, not Clinton, was in the White House when the 2001 bombing of the World Trade Center took place was probably one of al-Qaeda's great miscalculations. This is why, from all we can tell, al-Qaeda made an effort to defeat Bush in this election, something even Kerry seemed to suspect, hence his war-hawk transformation during the Democratic Convention.

12. Is President Bush's effort to make Iraq into a democracy feasible? Practically no one thinks that Islam and democracy are compatible. On the other hand, both American and Catholic theories hold that nations ought to be ruled with this form of rule, when possible, and that anyone can learn it with proper opportunity and instruction. It is certainly worth

a try, though it is not unreasonable to settle for something less. But the normal occurrence of democratic leaders being murdered when they do arise in such societies makes one very cautious.

13. The war is not against Iraq or Afghanistan as such but against al-Qaeda in any country that protects and harbors it. Without some sort of national protection in the Islamic world, this movement would have never gotten off the ground. Saudi Arabia is a particularly difficult problem because much of the current terrorist theory comes from the country's Wahhabi sect, while the oil money of the Saudi is used to finance, under freedom of religion, mosques and schools all over the world, including in the United States, that foster this radical version of Islam on the march. The House of Saud itself is in proximate danger of being taken over by this movement.

14. In today's ecumenical world, just about the only thing we hear about Islam is that it is a religion of peace, and that Jews, Christians, and Muslims worship the same God. The differences between what the religions hold are put on the back burner, in popular parlance, and the practice of Islam is practically unknown. Islam denies the two basic Christian positions, the Trinity and the Incarnation, and the version of the Bible in which these positions are established. This makes Christians dangerous enemies. Muslim states, following their own positions on the duty of state to religion, restrict in almost every way the religions within their borders. The state power is generally at the service of religion. The distinction of state and religion is unknown, when not considered blasphemous. The state is to foster the religion and suppress its enemies.

15. Historically, and even today, Muslim armies have attacked and occupied not only Christian lands, but those of Hindus, Buddhists, Chinese, and African tribes as well. Muslim armies came within an inch of conquering Western

Europe twice. Al-Qaeda Islam takes seriously its central notion that the world is intended by Allah to be Muslim. War is a legitimate means to accomplish this goal, and is, though it is difficult to comprehend, a spiritual tool.

16. Suicide bombing is a form of martyrdom. Such bombers have become a particularly effective weapon in recent decades, in part because of their effectiveness in causing chaos and in part as a deep expression of Muslim faith. Because such bombings violate almost every human instinct and principle, they are particularly difficult to handle both morally and militarily. They bring terror and war to everyone's bus stop. Indeed, suicide bombing may prove to be a much more lethal weapon than any of the unused nuclear weapons we have been worried about. If a nuclear weapon is used in some American or Western city, no doubt it will be set off by a suicide bomber who will consider himself a martyr. Likewise, like the September 11 pilots, he will be an intelligent man probably trained in how to use the weapon in some American or European school or university.

17. Religious opposition to war is based on a laudable preference for "peaceful" means, such as dialogue or unending negotiations. No dialogue is possible with this particular enemy except as a tactic to gain time. Religious leaders are not in charge of defending us in concrete situations. It is unfortunate in this case that religious leaders have not accurately seen the nature of this enemy, what it is capable of, and how and why it must be stopped, indeed of its religious motives. The older tradition in which religious leaders better understood the need, even for religion's sake, of a measured and adequate creation and use of force would have better served the only real peace that is possible as long as the world-conquering intention of al-Qaeda types is present and operative. Al-Qaeda is capable of operating from almost any point

in the world, including from American and European cities. It needs to be met where it is. This is a world war in that sense.

18. Can the United Nations handle this problem? If the UN had handled Iraq, Saddam would still be in power. Not a few would accept that. In some respects, the United Nations is part of the problem. The UN has no forces adequate to meet this particular challenge and no effective political will to do so. The United Nations Charter did not set up a world government but a place where problems might be discussed and, in certain carefully defined cases, acted upon. But it left to individual nations the major responsibility of effective action against movements that actually attacked other countries. The choice is not the United States with its allies or the United Nations. The alternative, in effect, is the United States or no effective action at all. Al-Qaeda leaders know this. This is why they would seek the weakest possible American government with a people least informed about what al-Qaeda really stands for.

19. One final time: this is a real war. The men who are responsible for attacking us consider us to be a decadent society whose influence would corrupt their peoples. They are not wholly wrong about this. What they seek is a religious goal, all the world subject to Allah. That is their peace. To accuse them of anything less is to do a disservice to them. This particular group will be stopped only by intelligent and adequate force. Military defeat leads to a theological crisis within Islam. At some level, the question of the truth of Islam has to be faced. It is not enough to say that we all worship the same God. If this is so, on their terms, there is no reason why the al-Qaeda dream should not conquer; indeed, their conquest would prove their point.

War Is Hell

Gregory D. Foster

from *Commonweal*

We do well to recall the words of General William Tecumseh Sherman. Having himself perpetrated an extraordinary amount of bloodshed and devastation, he warned all who might be given to bellicosity that "war is hell."

He prefaced that timeless observation by noting that "war is at best barbarism. . . . Its glory is all moonshine. It is only those who have neither fired a shot nor heard the shrieks and groans of the wounded who cry aloud for blood, more vengeance, more desolation." War is barbarism because it accomplishes nothing, at least nothing constructive or productive, that wouldn't be accomplished by other means. More to the point, war is moonshine because resorting to it signifies failure.

It is, first, a failure of diplomacy—the secretive, sweet-talking, arm-twisting deal making that politicians and career diplomats are supposed to be so good at but frequently aren't. It is a failure of intelligence, which—no matter how much money we throw at collecting and analyzing information on enemies, suspected and real—rarely predicts the conditions and events that precipitate war. War is a failure of imagination in effectively utilizing the many available instruments of foreign policy that offer alternatives to force. And it is a failure of strategic vision: an inability to discern underlying causes and unanticipated consequences, and an unwillingness to undertake preventive measures when they are needed.

When you've seen a comrade shot through the eye, and the back of his head blown off by an enemy bullet . . . When you've evacuated another, a ski instructor in regular life, whose legs have been blown off at the knee by a booby trap, and when you've visited him in the hospital but couldn't recognize him because his body was swollen to twice its normal size . . . When you've taken an enemy soldier's life and found a picture of his wife and child in his pocket . . . When you've tended moaning wounded all night who couldn't be evacuated because of enemy fire and the weather . . . When you've been trapped in the open by enemy mortar fire and couldn't find a place to hide . . . When you've lost your commander, the finest leader you've ever known, because his head was split open like a watermelon by the blade of a helicopter that an inept pilot couldn't control, and you've later offered feeble consolation to his widow and teenage son . . . When you've had a courageous comrade lose the use of his arm because friendly aircraft unloaded their ordnance too close to your position . . . When you've stood in front of your troops and tried reciting the names of their fallen comrades without showing emotion . . . When you've had to write even one of those letters to the parents of a dead soldier that begins "Dear Mr. and Mrs. Jones: It is with deepest sorrow that I write to express my sympathy over the loss of your son . . ."

When you've endured thirst, hunger, sleep deprivation, exhaustion, loneliness, fear, anger, sorrow, and pain; brain-frying heat, bone-chilling cold, soaking rain, debilitating mud, and choking dust; contaminated water and cold rations;

snakes, leeches, scorpions, and spiders; boils, dysentery, infection, and malaria; hostile fire and friendly fire . . .

When you've experienced such things, always for some higher cause that demands your unquestioning soldierly obedience despite—or because of—the frustrating ambiguity of the stakes involved . . . And then you consider that most politicians today who commit their nations to war have never donned a uniform or heard a shot fired in anger; that many of them assiduously avoided answering the call when it was their turn; that many of them, in turn, are among the most bellicose advocates of war . . . And then you consider that the same politicians, casually employing the duplicitous rhetoric of "national interest," "national survival," "clear and present danger," "urgency," and "necessity," are only too willing to risk the lives of others for their own ulterior political motives . . . And then you consider that, in committing forces to war without formal declaration, as they are wont to do, they regularly undercut the Constitution the military is sworn to support and defend . . .

Then you know something about the barbarity and stupidity of war.

Too bad so many of us don't get it.

Pilgrims
(In Spite of Ourselves)

Paul Elie

from *Boston College Magazine*

The day after John F. Kennedy was assassinated, Flannery O'Connor wrote a letter to her friend Sally Fitzgerald, who was living abroad at the time. "The President's death has cut up the country pretty bad," she reported. "All commercial television is stopped until after the funeral and even the football games are called off, which is about the extremest sign of grief possible."

In some ways it's a characteristic O'Connor remark: funny, unsentimental, informal, regional in emphasis. Here was a writer who could make a joke, and an insightful one, about the grisly death of a president. But it's also a remark that's instructive in what it does not say. Writing to a friend, a Catholic like herself and a Fitzgerald to boot, O'Connor says nothing about good and evil, nothing about the dashed expectations of American Catholics, nothing about the images of crucifixion and martyrdom the killing had called forth in the press. Here was a writer who knew better than to look for signs of the times in the usual places. Better to find them in the interrupted rituals of football and TV.

I was led to recall that remark earlier this year, when, as Lent began, a Lent that promised once again to be thick with news reports about controversy among Catholics—this time over Mel Gibson's film dramatization of the Passion—I found myself thinking about, and then writing about, the signs of the times in a short story that has little to do with Catholics or Catholicism.

The story, by Jhumpa Lahiri, is "This Blessed House," from *Interpreter of Maladies,* which won a Pulitzer prize a few years back. Like the other stories in the book, "This Blessed House" is about young people of Indian descent making lives for themselves in America. In this case they are newlyweds. Sanjeev, born in Calcutta, is an MIT-trained engineer. Tanima—nicknamed Twinkle during her girlhood in California—is a graduate student in English. Their marriage was arranged by their parents. So was their wedding, a party for friends and relatives, many of whom they'd never met. So was their honeymoon, a journey through India and its traditions, from which these "good little Hindus," as Twinkle calls them, are estranged.

As the story opens, the newlyweds are moving into a grand old house in Connecticut. It has fireplaces and an elegant staircase, and also some furnishings they didn't expect to find. A porcelain effigy of Christ tucked away in a cupboard above the stove. A "blond, unbearded Jesus delivering a sermon on a mountaintop." A "larger-than-life-sized watercolor poster of Christ, weeping translucent tears the size of peanut shells." A "3-D postcard of Saint Francis . . .taped to the back of the medicine cabinet." And, hiding behind an overgrown forsythia bush, "a blue plaster Virgin Mary as tall as their waists, with a blue painted hood draped over her head in the manner of an Indian bride."

The action of "This Blessed House" has to do with how two "good little Hindus" come to terms with the "sizable collection of Christian paraphernalia" that now belongs to them. As the story begins, these devotional objects are an offense to the engineer husband and a curiosity to the literary-critical wife. As the story develops, the objects come to seem something like blessed—and the newlyweds' encounter with them is what turns an arranged marriage into a real marriage.

As I read the story, though, I found myself wondering why those Christian objects were left behind in the first place, and what their presence suggested about the nature of the previous owners' faith.

Maybe the people who moved out of the house left Jesus, Mary, and the saints behind as a way of abandoning them, shaking the dust of Catholic culture off their boots.

Or maybe they left the religious figures in place out of respect—as if, after many years in the house, Jesus and Mary and St. Francis had become indigenous to the house, part of the landscape.

Or maybe they left in a hurry and could take only the possessions they considered essential—and found that Jesus and Mary and their plaster-of-Paris cohorts weren't essential.

Maybe they died and took their faith with them.

The story isn't about the religious faith of the people who used to live in that house. It isn't a story about religion at all. But I have midrashed the story at some length because it seems to me that the significance of those objects, the charge they give off to the reader, might tell us something about the beliefs of American Catholics today.

In these early years of the twenty-first century—which, if you count back to Columbus, is the seventh century in which there has been a Catholic presence in the Americas—it is hard to say whether the religious faith of American Catholics is something being cast off and left behind; something accepted, even taken for granted, as part of the landscape; or something with a powerful but indeterminate religious charge, now sacred, now profane, depending on the circumstances.

For the people who would lead American Catholics, a lack of certainty on this point is a problem, and one for which, these leaders often suggest, American Catholics themselves are especially to blame.

For the Catholic writer, however, this lack of certainty is the occasion for conflict, and so the source of drama, for this writer has been forced to recognize that it is in the quandaries of the would-be believer that the characteristic religious experience of our time is to be found—in the gropings of people who realize, often in the unlikeliest of circumstances, that they are believers in spite of themselves.

I am the author of a book about four great American Catholics of the last century: Dorothy Day, foundress of the Catholic Worker movement and editor of its newspaper; Thomas Merton, the Trappist monk and ceaseless chronicler of the inner life of the contemplative; Walker Percy, novelist, philosopher, and last gentleman of the South; and Flannery O'Connor, the "Christ-haunted" literary prodigy whose work has become the gold standard for Catholic fiction in its time.

The book, *The Life You Save May Be Your Own,* is about their lives and works and the way these seem in retrospect to converge in the middle of the last century, so that their four pilgrimages seem aspects of a single pilgrimage—from the God-obsessed past of Dante and Dostoyevsky out into the thrilling chaos of postwar America.

Pilgrimage is a motif that runs all through their work, from Dorothy Day's long-running *Catholic Worker* column called "On Pilgrimage" to the biography of Walker Percy called *A Pilgrim in the Ruins,* but as I sought to tell the story of their pilgrimage I found no one clear expression of what a pilgrimage is. So I searched their lives and their books and came up with a working idea, and it is this:

A pilgrimage is a journey taken in light of a story. The story precedes us: we've read it, we've heard it, we've been raised in it, in many instances. And at some point we need to test that story with our own experience—to read it with our lives and make it our own.

A pilgrimage—whether Dante's or our own—has certain distinguishing features. The pilgrim sets out on a path that others have taken, hoping to witness what others have seen—to see it with his or her own eyes. Pilgrims travel in company, but each must encounter the holy site personally. Finally, the pilgrims, on their return, tell others what they have seen and heard, so that others might be moved to set out on pilgrimages themselves—to go and do likewise.

The Life You Save May Be Your Own, then, is the story of a pilgrimage in which four writers took the models of European Christianity—which they found expressed most powerfully in certain great books—and made them their own in the circumstances of twentieth-century America. But it is also the story of the pilgrimage of American Catholics as a whole—about the diverse ways in which the pattern of pilgrimage runs through the life of the church and through our individual lives.

I have had the good fortune to be invited to speak about the book at events around the country, and inevitably two questions arise. One is this: Who are those four writers' successors—or to put it differently, why don't they have any successors? How can it be that their pilgrimage came to an end so abruptly?

Now, they obviously do have successors—the American Catholics who came of age in the time of the Second Vatican Council. And on the face of it there is plenty of evidence that the pilgrimage is still ongoing: the church is actually growing,

American Catholics have kept faith in an extraordinary variety of ways, and there is no shortage of writers with something to say about this or that aspect of the so-called American Catholic experience.

But to judge from my encounters with readers at those book events, there is no denying that as the American Catholics who were raised before the Second Vatican Council ponder last things, one's sense of an ending is strong.

If a certain pilgrimage, an epoch in the history of the church in these parts, is now coming to an end, it is the pilgrimage that had Vatican II at its center. And, that being the case, the sense of an ending is all the stronger, because it was with Vatican II that—doctrinally speaking—the church finally entered history, as the council fathers countered several centuries of dogma that situated the church above history with the affirmation that the church is the "people of God" on a pilgrimage in time—as the Lord's command to bring the Good News to the ends of the earth takes root among diverse peoples in particular eras and societies.

And yet the practical effect of the church's entry into history—in America, at least—was paradoxical and bewildering. Catholics actually became estranged from their history.

The council may have been a "return to the sources" of Catholic thought and life, but in this country, at least, it was welcomed as a new thing altogether. In a stroke the immigrant church was done away with, the Catholic children of the baby boom came of age, and a new and up-to-date American Catholicism was put in place.

So it was, evidently, for the people who came of age in the 1960s, and who have left us countless novels and memoirs about the experience. But for many of us who came of age later, the council seemed to have reduced the long Catholic past to an assemblage of 3-D St. Francises and watercolor Jesuses weeping translucent tears—and to have banished it all to the attic. A sense of the distance between the Catholic past and the Catholic present became a defining aspect of our religious experience. Religious life, for this generation, became a kind of wire-walk across the gap between history and experience.

Now, many people would say that this state of things has been arrested by the present pope. Yet John Paul also is a member of the Vatican II generation: exactly half of his life has passed on each side of the council. And his sense of history, too, can be paradoxical and bewildering. He has energetically reaffirmed teachings that seem defiant of history, or not cognizant of it. He is not immune to the old-world tendency to lord history over us new-world naïfs. And his long public decline has only heightened the sense of an ending—of a loss of vigor in the church in general.

The characters of Jhumpa Lahiri's story were raised, as I was, in the years after Vatican II, and the story plays on the comic mismatch of the European Catholic past and the American Catholic present in the way so much recent Catholic fiction does. But because Sanjeev and Twinkle are "good little Hindus" and not, say, Boston Irish Catholics, the story calls our attention to some profound changes in American religious life that the conciliar coming-of-age story can obscure.

One is the extent to which American society has changed in the past thirty-five years, with striking effects in the life of the churches. The writer Richard Rodriguez, for example, depicts the middle sixties—the Vatican II years—as crucial years in his story of the "browning" of America, a change that had more to do with immigration from without than assimilation from within. In Rodriguez's account, 1965 was the year when U.S. immigration laws were changed in such a way as to call forth several million immigrants from Asia—the likes of Sanjeev and Twinkle among them.

For these immigrants, Vatican II American Catholicism is not a new thing, not a suddenly formidable rival to Protestantism, not a cure for all the ills of the immigrant church or a watering down of ancient orthodoxy. For them, it is simply the local expression of the native religion.

That this is so is the result of another great change: the emergence of the Catholic Church as the dominant Christian body in the United States. Just when American Catholics were leaving their religious history behind, American Catholicism was becoming a fixture in the country's religious landscape.

This change is especially apparent in New England, where for two centuries, to speak of immigrants was to speak of Catholics, and to speak of pilgrimage was to speak of the Pilgrims. But things have changed. The Catholic faith has become indigenous in New England, to the point where reporters describing the recent scandal in the church referred reflexively to its effects in "Catholic Boston."

And in that change, perhaps, is found the answer to the other question I have been asked these past few months in connection with my book: How does the pilgrimage of the four writers bear on the crisis in the church today? What can they tell us about the scandal of priestly sexual abuse and the cover-up by the bishops?

I can't speak for those writers, only for this one. And it is my view that the scandal will inform the pilgrimage of today's American Catholics the way the Second Vatican Council did the pilgrimage of the generation before ours.

Not so long ago I might have stood here and told you that the American Catholics of today were akin to the "good little Hindus" of "This Blessed House"—that for many of us Catholicism seems like somebody else's religion. Its previous owners have left in haste and disarray. Its sacred images are encountered inadvertently and against one's will, now threatening, now bewildering, now kitschy, now a source of the genuine curiosity that can prompt an indifferent husband to feel, in the presence of his new bride and the sacred images that have caught her fancy, "as if the world contained hidden wonders he could not anticipate, or see."

I might have told you, in short, that American Catholics more than ever were estranged from their history.

Well, we are now in a different age and facing a different predicament. And the difference is this. With the scandal of priestly sexual abuse, the American Catholics of today have entered history at last. The exciting story of an ecumenical council and its aftermath has been interrupted once and for all, pushed aside by a story so appalling, so contrary to all that is true in Christian faith and practice, that it calls faith and practice into question.

No longer are American Catholics today akin to those "good little Hindus," looking with detached curiosity on the canonical images of modern Catholic kitsch. We are more like the people who left that grand old house in disarray. Some of us have abandoned faith in disgust and astonishment, have died to the spirit once and for all. Some of us have left the Catholic furniture in place, part of the landscape, even though, in truth, we have moved on. Some of us, contrariwise, have kept faith but left behind the appurtenances of American Catholic belief. And yet some of us have discovered, in our betrayal and sense of violation, that our Catholic faith goes deeper toward the core of ourselves than we had suspected.

Whereas Vatican II was characterized by a domestic image—the "opening of the windows"—our entry into history today is characterized by images of flight. For this writer, two such images stand out, joined together in a kind of diptych. One is the image of Boston's cardinal archbishop dining out in a restaurant in Rome—having caught a flight out of Logan for the weekend—when he was said to be on solitary retreat in New England praying over his predicament. The other is the image of a man, a victim of priestly sexual abuse, absorbed in prayer behind the steering wheel at a traffic light, for, as he told a reporter for the *New York Times,* he no longer feels safe praying in the church, or anywhere except "in my vehicle."

The leader of the bishops' conference recently characterized the priestly sexual abuse scandal as "history." So it is, but not in the sense he meant. It is not past; it is a provocation and a point of departure.

Those who would lead the church are concerned about the scandal's long-term effects. But the Catholic writer knows that these effects are not to be assessed sociologically and in aggregate—in terms of parish affiliation, annual giving patterns, and the like—but are to be contemplated and dramatized, one would-be believer at a time.

With that in mind, this writer can see that an encounter with the church at a low point in its history is not necessarily unfortunate. For one thing, there are plenty of other low points in the church's history, and any genuine Catholic faith must take account of them.

For another—and this is the heart of the matter—the scandal has made apparent that many of the American Catholics of today have been living on the faith of our predecessors. Now we have begun, with weeping and gnashing of teeth, to encounter this faith tradition for ourselves, so that we might make it our own, whatever the consequences. The would-be believer of this generation hasn't lost her faith so much as her fideism, her willingness to take faith itself on faith.

When *The Moviegoer* won the National Book Award, Walker Percy was asked why there were so many good Southern writers. "Because we lost the War," he said, and Flannery O'Connor later glossed his remark with startling eloquence. "What he was saying is that we have had our Fall," she explained. "We have gone into the world with an inburnt sense of human limitations, and with a sense of mystery that could not have developed sufficiently in the rest of the country."

And so it may be today. I suspect that the scandal has in its sad and wounding way sent today's Catholics back to the sources of religious faith, much the way the council did our predecessors. Is there a God? What might it mean that God came to earth, lived, died, and rose again? What might it mean to follow him?

For this generation the pattern of pilgrimage is not the one suggested by Pentecost, after which the disciples went forth to bring the Good News to all the nations, each in his own language. It is the pattern of Lent. We begin literally at the bottom, as dust, humbled, broken, and divided, and venture forth from there. Instead of measuring our lives and the life of the church today against the success story of the American Catholic coming-of-age, we must measure them against the Gospel story, which is a story of failure, of division, of violence.

A new age requires a new pilgrimage. But it seems to me that today's Catholics might look for example to the great pilgrims of the era that led up to the Second Vatican Council—to Dorothy Day, Thomas Merton, Walker Percy, and Flannery O'Connor, who found and kept Catholic faith by making it their own.

For one thing, those writers' lives and works remind us that the business of the Christian believer, first of all, is not to fix the church, not to change the church, but to follow Christ: to discern the pattern of Christian pilgrimage in our individual lives and to act upon it accordingly. They prompt us to ask: On the church's "pilgrimage in time," what paths are our individual pilgrimages meant to take? What will the varieties of twenty-first century Catholic experience be? What might a life of holiness or sanctity look like?

At the same time, those writers remind us that religious experience is not merely subjective, and that the Christian story—so Catholics believe—is not just a story but a true story, a work of nonfiction.

For those writers, it was a matter of conviction that as human beings all of us have the pattern of pilgrimage inscribed within us—that just as the word *history* contains *story* within it, so our earthly pilgrimage contains story within it, so our earthly pilgrimage contains the image of Christ as its root or end.

Dorothy Day's charity and her pacifism both stemmed from her belief that in the stranger, in every stranger, friend or foe, the image of Christ is found.

Walker Percy found the basis of his faith in what he called the "Christian anthropology"—the church's understanding of the human person as a creature at once broken and fixed.

Thomas Merton described the "disintegrated wandering" that comes about when the outer pilgrimage does not correspond to the inner one, a journey to the encounter with the living God in contemplative prayer, the experience toward which, he believed, human nature is oriented.

Flannery O'Connor found an image of this belief in her story "Parker's Back," in which a man has a Byzantine Christ tattooed into his back in acknowledgment that he is made in the image of God.

Catholics believe that every human person is inscribed with the image of God, and that in some sense we are all on pilgrimage together, bound for a common destination. This is another way of saying that the Christian story is not only a true story; it is also a story—so we believe—that everybody ought to know, for each of our pilgrimages must pass, will pass, whether we like it or not, by the foot of the cross.

By these lights, the "good little Hindus" who move into the house are inscribed with the image of God no less than the Catholics who moved out, and the image of that blessed house with figures of Christ and Mary and the saints in the corners is akin to the Catholic image of the human soul.

In my experience, the church's claim to be the bearer of salvation for all is the hardest of all the hard sayings. It is this claim, as much as the sins of the priests and bishops, that makes our religion scandalous to the American Catholic of today.

Only a true naïf would hope that the American Catholics of today might somehow overcome this double stumbling block—the scandal in the church and the scandal of faith— without conflict and anguish. And yet only a naïf would think that the image of God on which our pilgrimage depends—an image inscribed by an Other and made vivid by culture— could be blotted out altogether by scandal.

It may be that the would-be believer will never become a believer—that the flight of American Catholics today will never turn into a genuine pilgrimage. It may be that today's American Catholics will remain pilgrims in spite of ourselves, oriented toward a destination of which we are unaware or indifferent or openly disdainful, even as it promises to make the difference between our lives being saved and merely being survived or salvaged.

Only a cynic would hope for such an outcome. But only a cynic—one of a different kind—would presume to say that the terrible events of recent years have been good for the church in this country, that they are something like—I have heard it said—an occasion of grace. For one thing, the granting of grace is out of our hands. For another, it is too soon to tell: although the hour is late, the pilgrimage of today's American Catholics is only just beginning.

Is It Not Possible to Be Radical and Not Atheist?

Dorothy Day

from *The Catholic Worker*

For those who are sitting on park benches in the warm spring sunlight.

For those who are huddling in shelters trying to escape the rain.

For those who are walking the streets in the all but futile search for work.

For those who think that there is no hope for the future, no recognition of their plight—this little paper is addressed.

It is printed to call their attention to the fact that the Catholic Church has a social program—to let them know that there are people of God who are working for not only their spiritual but also their material welfare.

It's time there was a Catholic paper printed for the unemployed.

The fundamental aim of most radical sheets is the conversion of its readers to radicalism and atheism.

Is it not possible to be radical and not atheist?

Is it not possible to protest, to expose, to complain, to point out abuses and demand reforms without desiring the overthrow of religion?

In an attempt to popularize and make known the encyclicals of popes in regard to social justice and the program put forth by the church for the "reconstruction of the social order," this news sheet, the *Catholic Worker,* is started.

It is not yet known whether it will be a monthly, a fortnightly, or a weekly. It all depends on the funds collected for the printing and distribution. Those who can donate are asked to do so.

This first number of the *Catholic Worker* was planned, written, and edited in the kitchen of a tenement on Fifteenth Street, on subway platforms, on the train, on the ferry.

There is no editorial office, no salaries paid.

The money for the printing of the first issue was raised by begging small contributions from friends. A priest in Newark sent us ten dollars and the prayers of his congregation. A sister in New Jersey, garbed also in holy poverty, sent us a dollar. Another kindly and generous friend sent twenty-five. The rest of it the editors squeezed out of their own earnings, and, at that, they were using money necessary to pay milk bills, gas bills, electric bills.

By accepting delay, the utilities did not know that they were furthering the cause of social justice. They were, for the time being, unwitting cooperators.

Next month someone may donate us an office. Who knows?

It is cheering to remember that Jesus Christ wandered this earth with no place to lay his head. *The foxes have holes and the birds have their nests, but the Son of Man has no place to lay his head.* And when we consider our fly-by-night existence, our uncertainty, we remember (with pride at sharing the honor) that the disciples supped by the seashore and wandered through cornfields picking the ears from the stalks wherewith to make frugal meals.

Mourning and Remembrance

George Weigel

from *The Wall Street Journal*

He once described his high school years as a time in which he was "completely absorbed" by a passion for the theater. So it was fitting that Karol Józef Wojtyla lived a very dramatic life. As a young man, he risked summary execution by leading clandestine acts of cultural resistance to the Nazi occupation of Poland. As a fledgling priest, he adopted a Stalin-era nom de guerre—Wujek, "Uncle"—while creating zones of intellectual and spiritual freedom for college students; those students, now older men and women themselves, called him Wujek to the end. As archbishop of Kraków, he successfully fought the attempt by Poland's Communist overseers to erase the nation's cultural memory. As Pope John Paul II, he came back to Poland in June 1979, and over nine days during which the history of the twentieth century pivoted he ignited a revolution of conscience that helped make possible the collapse of European communism a decade later.

Evangelical Witness

The world will remember the drama of this life in the days ahead, even as it measures John Paul II's many other accomplishments: his transformation of the papacy from a managerial office to one of evangelical witness; his voluminous teaching, touching virtually every aspect of contemporary life; his dogged pursuit of Christian unity; his success in blocking the Clinton administration's efforts to have abortion on demand declared a basic human right; his remarkable magnetism for young people; his groundbreaking initiatives with Judaism; his robust defense of religious freedom as the first of human rights.

And in the remembering, certain unforgettable images will come to mind: the young pope bouncing infants in the air, and the old pope bowed in remembrance over the memorial flame at Yad Vashem, Jerusalem's Holocaust memorial; the pope wearing a Kenyan tribal chieftain's feathered crown; the pope waving his papal cross in defiance of Sandinista demonstrators in Managua; the pope skiing; the pope lost in prayer in countless venues; the pope kneeling at the grave of murdered Solidarity chaplain Jerzy Popieluszko; the pope slumped in pain in the popemobile seconds after taking two shots from a 9mm semiautomatic—and the pope counseling and encouraging the would-be assassin in his Roman prison cell.

Some will dismiss him as hopelessly "conservative" in matters of doctrine and morals, although it is not clear how religious and moral truth can be parsed in liberal/conservative terms. The shadows cast upon his papacy by clerical scandal and the misgovernance of some bishops will focus others' attention. John Paul II was the most visible human being in history, having been seen live by more men and women than any other man who ever lived; the remarkable thing is that millions of those people, who saw him only at a great distance, will think they have lost a friend. Those who knew him more intimately experience today a profound sense of personal loss at the death of a man who was so wonderfully, thoroughly, engagingly human—a man of intelligence and wit and courage whose humanity breathed integrity and sanctity.

So there are many ways of remembering and mourning him. Pope John Paul II should also be remembered, however, as a man with a penetrating insight into the currents that flow beneath the surface of history, currents that in fact create history, often in surprising ways.

In a 1968 letter to the French Jesuit theologian Henri de Lubac, then-cardinal Karol Wojtyla suggested that "a degradation, indeed a pulverization, of the fundamental uniqueness of each human person" was at the root of the twentieth century's grim record: two world wars, Auschwitz and the Gulag, a cold war threatening global disaster, oceans of blood and mountains of corpses. How had a century begun with such high hopes for the human future produced humankind's greatest catastrophes? Because, Karol Wojtyla proposed, Western humanism had gone off the rails, collapsing into forms of self-absorption, and then self-doubt, so severe that men and women had begun to wonder whether there was any truth at all to be found in the world, or in themselves.

This profound crisis of culture, this crisis in the very idea of the human, had manifested itself in the serial crises that had marched across the surface of contemporary history, leaving carnage in their wake. But unlike some truly "conservative" critics of late modernity, Wojtyla's counterproposal was not rollback; rather, it was a truer, nobler humanism, built on the foundation of the biblical conviction that God had made the human creature in his image and likeness, with intelligence and free will, a creature capable of knowing the good and freely choosing it. That, John Paul II insisted in a vast number of variations on one great theme, was the true measure of man—the human capacity, in cooperation with God's grace, for heroic virtue.

Here was an idea with consequences, and the pope applied it to effect across a broad spectrum of issues.

One variant form of debased humanism was the notion that "history" is driven by the politics of willfulness (the Jacobin heresy) or by economics (the Marxist heresy). During his epic pilgrimage to Poland in June 1979, at a moment when "history" seemed frozen and Europe permanently divided into hostile camps, John Paul II demonstrated that "history" worked differently, because human beings aren't just the by-products of politics or economics. He gave back to his people their authentic history and culture—their identity. And in doing so, he gave them tools of resistance that Communist truncheons could not reach. Fourteen months after teaching that great lesson in dignity, the pope watched and guided the emergence of Solidarity. And then the entire world began to see the Communist tide recede, like the slow retreat of a plague.

After the cold war, when more than a few analysts and politicians were in a state of barely restrained euphoria, imagining a golden age of inevitable progress for the cause of political and economic freedom, John Paul II saw more deeply and clearly. He quickly decoded new threats to what he had called, in that 1968 letter to Father Lubac, the "inviolable mystery of the human person," and so he spent much of the 1990s explaining that freedom untethered from moral truth risks self-destruction.

For if there is only your truth and my truth and neither one of us recognizes a transcendent moral standard (call it "the truth") by which to settle our differences, then either you will impose your power on me or I will impose my power on you; Nietzsche, great, mad prophet of the twentieth century, got at least that right. Freedom uncoupled from truth, John Paul taught, leads to chaos and thence to new forms of tyranny. For in the face of chaos (or fear), raw power will inexorably replace persuasion, compromise, and agreement as the coin of the political realm. The false humanism of freedom misconstrued as "I did it my way" inevitably leads to freedom's decay, and then to freedom's self-cannibalization. This was not the soured warning of an antimodern scold; this was the sage counsel of a man who had given his life to freedom's cause from 1939 on.

Thus the key to the freedom project in the twenty-first century, John Paul urged, lay in the realm of culture: in a vibrant public moral culture capable of disciplining and directing the tremendous energies—economic, political, aesthetic, and, yes, sexual—set loose in free societies. A vibrant public moral culture is essential for democracy and the market, for only such a culture can inculcate and affirm the virtues necessary to make freedom work. Democracy and the free economy, he taught in his 1991 encyclical *Centesimus Annus,* are goods, but they are not machines that can cheerfully run by themselves. Building the free society certainly involves getting the institutions right; beyond that, however, freedom's future depends on men and women of virtue, capable of knowing, and choosing, the genuinely good.

Future of Freedom

That is why John Paul II relentlessly preached genuine tolerance: not the tolerance of indifference, as if differences over the good didn't matter, but the real tolerance of differences engaged, explored, and debated within the bond of a profound respect for the humanity of the other. Many were puzzled that this pope, so vigorous in defending the truths of Catholic faith, could become, over a quarter century, the world's premier icon of religious freedom and interreligious civility. But here, too, John Paul II was teaching a crucial lesson about the future of freedom: universal empathy comes through, not around, particular convictions. There is no Rawlsian veil of ignorance behind which the world can withdraw, to subsequently emerge with decency in its pocket.

There is only history. But that history, the pope believed, is the story of God's quest for man, and man then taking the same path as God. "History" is his-story. Believing that, Karol Józef Wojtyla, Pope John Paul II, changed history. The power of his belief empowered millions of others to do the same.

Brutally Real

Mark Bosco, SJ

from *Commonweal*

When I was leaving the Jesuit novitiate and was assigned to teach high school, my novice master told me: "Remember St. Ignatius's dictum: always go in their door and bring them out yours."

Although I am now a university professor, the phrase has been with me during a Lenten and Easter season in which the main topic of conversation has been Mel Gibson's *Passion of the Christ*. Whether with friends, family, or colleagues, it seems that all of us must go through a ritual conversation on the film. There have been hundreds of articles on *The Passion* in the secular and religious press, each with a bit of new information or an interesting critical perspective. Many have been helpful in articulating the theological and aesthetic strengths and weaknesses of the film.

My university recently held an excellent panel discussion on *The Passion,* during which a Bible scholar critiqued the film's historical and scriptural accuracy, a Jewish professor responded to the film's alleged anti-Semitism, and two doctoral students in theology—an evangelical Christian minister and a Catholic laywoman—offered their own thoughts. (He praised it, albeit with reservations, while she was very disturbed by it.) The panel was well attended by undergraduates and some neighbors from around the university. During the question period, most of the student audience voiced strong, positive reactions to the film that often seemed at odds with the critical tone of the scholarly participants. Although the panel's conclusions—that the movie is not biblically accurate, that it at least flirts with anti-Semitism, that it overindulges in violence—seemed sound to me, I wondered why the panelists' remarks were so out of sync with the experience of most of the students.

As I continued the discussion in the classroom, it was obvious that my students couldn't understand why the criticism of the film failed to recognize that it was, in one student's words, "a sacred event" in their lives. They didn't want to hear what was wrong with the film but challenged me to articulate why it was so popular with young people.

I began wondering, Why does Generation Y (those born after 1981) see this film so differently from their elders? Is there a way for me, a thirty-nine-year-old professor of English and theology, to go in their cultural door and bring them out my own?

This led to a class project. I asked my students a range of questions about the film, from the portrayal of Mary, Jesus, Judas, and Satan to its alleged anti-Semitism. What follows is a summation of some of their more articulate responses to three questions: Was it a spiritual experience for you? What do you make of the violence? How do you make sense of the aesthetics of the film?

It is clear that for most of these students Gibson's rendition of the Passion was a spiritual experience. All but a few students noted how deeply moved they were while watching it.

"I doubt that seeing it will make converts," wrote one, "but its sheer in-your-face force has the power to renew one's faith."

Another added, "It didn't teach me much about Jesus—I already knew the story—but it did succeed in making me present to the story in ways that I might never have been."

And one wrote, "Although I am a Muslim student and do not view Christ in the same light as Christians, I was deeply moved by the violence that befell Christ."

For many of these students, the film was analogous to a liturgical experience. They saw it more as a ritual than a biblical history lesson. Catholic film critics and theologians have commented on how closely the film resembles medieval Passion plays or the Catholic devotion of the stations of the cross, a ritual that many older Catholics grew up performing during Lent.

Cinematically, the film invites the viewer on the same journey. A young woman made this connection in an e-mail: "My youth group in high school put on performances of the stations of the cross. I often noticed that the older members of the church were moved and touched more by the story we were acting than the younger members of the parish. . . .[So] I think it was watching the violence in *The Passion* that helped me get deeper into the story in a way that I never had before."

This sense of the film as "liturgical" was highlighted by a young man who had made two Kairos retreats at his Jesuit high school. He noted that "the film was like Kairos, as if we were in God's time. It seemed like time had stopped. When the film ended I had no idea that over two hours had passed. It felt like half an hour."

Most interesting were responses to the violence in *The Passion,* especially the twenty-minute scourging scene. A young man noted, "The scene was very draining to watch and

I was unable to stomach some parts of it, and I am a guy used to watching gory, violent movies. It borders on the sadistic because most movie violence doesn't deal with a completely defenseless person being beaten half to death."

A young woman went further, claiming, "I have been desensitized to some degree by the amount of violence I've been shown throughout my life. Movie violence has progressively increased to thrill and heighten the shock value in order to keep our appetites satisfied."

Why then, she asked, was this film's violence different?

"If *The Passion* were completely fiction, I wouldn't care much about the violence," she said. "I would have compared the thirty-nine lashes to the decapitations I saw in *Kill Bill* and the gruesome murders in *Pulp Fiction*. But the impact of this violence is different—Christ was scourged, Christ was brutalized."

Gibson's use of violence seems to be the primary reason why these students found the film engrossing. The violence took them somewhere, moved them in some way. In a recent *New York Times* essay, novelist Mary Gordon noted that the film's screenwriter, Benedict Fitzgerald, is the son of the late Sally Fitzgerald; his mother had been the great friend, editor, and biographer of Flannery O'Connor, that most Catholic of modernists who used violence and the grotesque to deconstruct modern assumptions about religious faith and belief. Through violence, O'Connor was able to startle the reader into seeing a new and soberer vision of God's grace at work. O'Connor insisted that her use of violence was "strangely capable of returning my characters to reality and preparing them to accept their moment of grace." My students recognized just such an aesthetic in *The Passion*—though when asked to describe it, they were at pains to articulate what exactly it might mean.

Most students said that the usual presentation of violence in movies and television left them unprepared for the focused, violent confrontations in Gibson's film. One junior noted that "having grown up with a kind of cleaned-up, Hanna-Barbera version of the passion of Jesus during my Catholic grade school and high school education, it was at first hard to watch something this realistic. At the same time, it made me realize how brutal Christ's scourging and crucifixion were."

Another student stated bluntly: "I don't know why there is such a fuss over the violence. If there is too much blood in this film, then there is too much blood in the Bible. If we can see mountains of bodies and rivers of blood in Hollywood movies whose purpose seems to be to glorify violence as a part of life, then it seems obvious that the violence in [this film] indicts such violence."

One conclusion, at least for these students, is that Gibson's aesthetic is not over-the-top, not violence as mere spectacle. Though an older generation may find Gibson's use of violence overbearing and indulgent, many younger people see it as part of the cultural zeitgeist.

One of the most interesting and thoughtful responses on the violence in the film came from a sophomore who dubbed Gibson's vision an "aesthetic of brutal realism." He noted, "The violence tears away all other emotions you might get out of violence in our culture. It is focused on one person, and there is no way it can be entertaining. If it starts out as a thrill, it quickly moves to shock, and you're left with only a terrible sense of sadness, of loss. The only thing left for you to do is to stay watching, to bear witness."

There is something profoundly true in this statement. The dramatic depiction of violence is part of the cultural experience of many young people. It thrills, shocks, and entertains, but usually from the safe, ironic distance of print, film, or video games. Gibson's *Passion* is a bloodied tragedy that has never before been so compellingly realized on film. There is little space for a postmodern, ironic gaze; instead, the viewer is asked to stand and watch. For several students, that meant watching the movie through Mary's eyes.

"Mary helped put a personality to Jesus more than any other character in the film," a senior wrote. "We enter from her position. She is there from the beginning until the end of Jesus' life."

Added another: "Without Gibson panning to [Mary], it would have been hard to keep watching."

Whatever the cinematic merits, historical accuracy, or theological vision of the film, it must be said that it has made students think. Indeed, that seemed to be the only consensus among the respondents: "It really challenged my conceptions about redemption through suffering"; "I have never thought about this before"; "It made me think about my faith."

Mel Gibson's film has become a cultural phenomenon. It has done what many others have aspired to do: compelled young people to think about Good Friday in a whole new way. For a post–Vatican II generation that is not used to the stations of the cross or singing the Stabat Mater or sitting through long Lenten sermons on Christ's passion, Gibson's film is inspiring them to "keep watch" as it imaginatively refashions what previous generations of Catholics have taken for granted. *The Passion of the Christ* may just be another form of devotion for a new generation.

What Does Mel Gibson's Movie *Mean*?

Barbara Nicolosi

from Church of the Masses,
http://churchofthemasses.blogspot.com

Editor's note: Like most blog postings, the following is ragged; yet, like the best blogs, it also has a tart straightforwardness that we admire. Interesting medium, the blog: sort of a diary / letter / monologue / public square. It will be fun to see if this medium develops masters.

Wednesday, March 3, 2004

I will be participating in a panel discussion on *The Passion of the Christ* at the University of Southern California's Annenberg School for Communication this evening. I have seven minutes to lay out some of my thoughts regarding the project. Excuse me while I collect my thoughts here . . .

I thought I would work off the question above, distinguishing between what the project means to Hollywood, what it means to the masses who are flocking to it, and then what it means in itself.

What does the film mean to Hollywood?

The industry is shocked by the box-office numbers for the project. The day before *POTC* opened, I read one of the industry box-office pundits predicting that the film "might actually top $30 million in its opening week." Talk about misreading the signs of the times . . .

A lot of people in town were prepared to credit the original spike in box office to a campaign orchestrated by church groups. I don't think anyone can look at the $125 million in five days without the following thought process intruding: "Either there are a hell of a lot more church groups out there than I knew, or, more likely, there are a lot more people interested in Jesus out there than I ever imagined."

There are many in Hollywood who will want to dismiss *POTC* as a fluke. And they would be right. The primary thing that has powered this film is the fact that it was written, produced, directed, and bankrolled by a global movie superstar. We have grown so used to movie stars being preoccupied with saving whales, wearing ribbons, and ridiculing religion that the notion of one of "that tribe" producing a devout consideration of the redemptive sacrifice of Jesus is truly inconceivable.

People want to know what the success of this film will mean in terms of future projects. Who knows? It might mean some openness for biblical epics, but the problem is that you aren't going to see another *POTC* until you have a filmmaker who actually believes and loves the biblical story. *POTC* is awesome because of its theological sophistication. This kind of movie could only be produced by a filmmaker who is in awe of God. I don't know that there are too many other A-list directors who could meet that requirement.

What does **POTC** mean to viewers?

This is another way of getting around to the two questions: "Does this film make viewers want to go beat up Jewish people?" and "Is the violence in this film ultimately sickening to the viewer?" The question comes down to "Is artistic license absolute?" or, in other words, "How much responsibility does an artist/entertainer bear in the impact their work has on their audience?"

Some thoughts about artistic freedom . . .

I belong to a school of thought that sees the arts as having a vital place in human society. Decorating stuff is more than just a private impulse for self-expression. But it is *minimally* that, and we have to leave room for the artist to make dark and crazy, weird things in the privacy of their own studios. The ethical question comes in when the artist decides to take some of that stuff out and put it in the middle of the public square. Some of the stuff that bursts out of the artist is poisonous to human society. It's like vomit. Vomit is very real. But reality isn't virtue enough to allow someone to smear it all over the walls in a room. A lot of the art we have been subjected to for the last century has been tantamount to vomit smeared on the wall.

The artist can lead people to want to be good. The arts can stretch us to see and experience further than our normal workaday worlds would allow. The arts can connect us to one another, to our deepest selves, and to the transcendent.

The artist's ethical question comes down to "Will this work of mine lead people toward the good or away from it?

Will it fill them with hope or despair? Will it make them want to be more fully human, or will it validate them in settling for being more like a pig?"

Now, the fact is that the artist's responsibility can only be measured according to the standard of a healthy human being. We can't limit the artist, for example, because some wacko out there has a pathological response to the color purple. This is what governments try to do, and it is always wrong. However, suppose *most* people have a pathological response to the color purple. Suppose it isn't aberrant to start frothing at the mouth when you see grape soda, but rather the norm for the kind of beings we are. Then the artist who uses purple is being irresponsible.

I don't think *POTC* leaves most people in a worse place than where they were before. I think it leaves most people better off. The fact that it is not a happy film doesn't say anything about this question at all. Sometimes truth is frightening and being disturbed is a positive, like being wakened from sleep.

Much of the criticism of *POTC* is hugely problematic in terms of the whole question of artistic freedom. Where are the people in the creative community for whom artistic freedom has been their clarion call?

Some thoughts about propaganda . . .

The anti-Semitism charges against *The Passion of the Christ* keep coming down to one of two notions:

1. *POTC* is anti-Semitic, or

2. While *POTC* is not in itself anti-Semitic, some people might find their latent strands of anti-Semitism affirmed by the film.

Regarding the first notion, I think that to be effective, propaganda must in some sense be intentional. Now, if Mel Gibson was trying to make an anti-Semitic work, he did a very bad job of it. In fact, we could go through the film and find ways in which hatred for Jewish people might have been heightened. There is just too much ambiguity in the film to claim that it has this agenda. So if this was the agenda of the film, we would have to conclude that it was very sloppily done.

Regarding the second notion, see the argument above about making art for people who have a pathological response to the color purple.

Some thoughts about artistic license ...

Mel is getting criticism from theological circles for making a film that is historically inaccurate in its sensibilities. Other people have issues with the fact that there are things in the movie that are not in the Scriptures. Mel has been going around claiming that he made a film that is as historical as possible, and faithful to the Scriptures.

This dispute reflects a distance in terms between the scholar and the artist. Mel has made a film that is visually historical. He got the costumes right. He got the production design right. The characters are Semitic-looking. They don't speak with British accents and have blue eyes and perfect teeth. The scholars want to see a dissertation on the relationship between Rome and its occupied territories, and specifically the situation in Palestine. That is the kind of complexity that belongs in books. That is why we have them.

There are three senses in which an artist can be inspired by the Scriptures.

The first sense would be in the attempt to be literal. (Enter evangelical America.) People tell me the movie *The Gospel of John* is like that. *Jesus,* the Jesus film that Protestants love so much, is probably also of this type.

The second sense would be in producing a work that is antiscriptural. That is, the artist creates a work that is at odds with the fundamental spirit of the work. He is arguing with the hierarchy set up in the Scriptures. Such a project would be *The Last Temptation of Christ.* Many people of faith find the character of Jesus in that film to be incompatible with the Jesus they know.

The third sense in which the artist can be inspired by Scripture is in functioning superscripturally. This involves the distortion of some details to achieve a new emphasis. The emphasis, however, is fully in concert with the fundamental spirit of the Scriptures. For example, the image of God's finger touching Adam's finger is nowhere in the Bible. However, it is absolutely consonant with the sense of the creation narrative. And, borrowing from Pope John Paul II, its very distortion becomes a source of theology.

The Passion of the Christ is most like this.

On another level, a lot of theologian types are angry at the story that *POTC* tells. They want the movie to be more about Jesus' preaching, or about the Resurrection. The only response to these people is a shrug. That isn't the movie that this artist wanted to make. He has the right to make whatever movie he wants to make as long as it ultimately leaves the viewers better off than they were before. To ask the sacred artist to create a work that encompasses the entire panoply of salvation history and theology is to bind up an impossible burden and lay it on the artist's palette.

For whom does **POTC** toll?

Clearly, the film is much more for people who know the story than for those who do not. Were it not, there would be a lot more attempts to give backstory and develop characters. The fact is that the film picks up like the stations of the cross on the wall of any church. And then it just goes. Some people could stroll into a church without knowing anything about Christianity and admire the craft of the sculptor or painter who created the stations of the cross. Some others might be provoked to learn more about the story that the stations signify. "Why is this man being done to death? Where are his friends? Why doesn't he fight back?" Finally, some will see something in one of the stations that will strike them at the bone. They will be stopped by one of the images, and it will be a moment of grace for them. Mel Gibson's *Passion* will probably work like that with different groups of non-Christians.

What about the violence?

The Passion of the Christ is not a great film *in spite of* its violence; it is a great film *through* its violence. The violence is the principal symbolic device of the piece. Personally, I thought he could have cut some of it out. But maybe for him the violence wasn't quite enough to express the horror of sin that he was getting at. The pope says that the artist will always look at his work and find it insufficient in light of the creative inspiration that has been given to him.

Two Poems

Paul Mariani

from *Deaths & Transfigurations: Poems*

Solar Ice

The sudden shock of what you really are.
Early March. The tentative return of the afternoons.
Saturday, and Mass again. The four.
All about swelling buds on beech & ash
& maples. Crocuses & snowdrops
trilling. Four months impacted ice at last
receding from the north side of the house,
and bobbing robins back & soon, soon, red-
winged blackbirds strutting on the lawn.
Soon too the sweet familiar groundswell
of peepers in the marshes. Reason
enough to melt the frozen heart.

Father lifted the host above his head & prayed:
a small white sun around which everything
seemed to coalesce, cohere & choir. But
as I raised my head, the thought
of some old insult likewise reared

its head, and in that instant the arctic
hatred flared, shutting out my world
& spring, along with, yes, my lovely wife & sons,
a no & no & yet another no, until I caught
myself refuse the proffered gift of Love.

At once the host diminished to a tiny o:
an empty cipher, like some solar disc
imploding on itself. Only my precious
hate remained, the self-salt taste
of some old wound rubbed raw again,
a jagged O at the center of my world.
Ah, so this is it, I whistled through my teeth.
So this is hell, or some lovely ether
foretaste of it, along at ninety north,
with darkness everywhere & ice, & ice
& ice & more ice on the way, and this
sweet abyss between myself & You.

Pietà

New Year's Eve, a party at my brother's.
Hats, favors, the whole shebang, as we waited
for one world to die into another.

And still it took three martinis before
she could bring herself to say it. How
the body of her grown son lay alone there

in the ward, just skin & bone, the nurses
masked & huddled in the doorway, afraid
to cross over into a world no one seemed

to understand. This was a dozen years ago,
you have to understand, before the thing
her boy had had become a household word.

Consider Martha. Consider Lazarus four days gone.
If only you'd been here, she says, *if only
you'd been here.* And no one now to comfort her,

no one except this priest, she says, an old
friend who'd stood beside them through the dark
night of it all, a bull-like man, skin black

as the black he wore, the only one who seemed
willing to walk across death's threshold into
that room. And now, she says, when the death

was over, to see him lift her son, light as a baby
with the changes death had wrought, and cradle him
like that, then sing him on his way, a cross

between a lullaby & blues, *mmm hmmm,* while
the nurses, still not understanding what they saw,
stayed outside and watched them from the door.

A Journalist's Calling

Don Wycliff

from *American Catholics and Civic Engagement*

I can as easily imagine myself not Catholic as I can imagine myself not black. Which is to say that I cannot imagine it at all.

I can't imagine not getting up on Sunday morning, going to my parish church, and sharing with my friends and neighbors there in the celebration of the Eucharist.

I can't imagine not having that mystical sense of connectedness with other Catholics all over the globe through the prayers and rituals and tradition and teaching of the church.

I can't imagine not thinking of life in terms of sin and grace and sacrifice and the cross and the Resurrection.

I can't imagine not thinking of the pope as the head of my church, the Vicar of Christ, the principal teacher and shepherd of the faithful.

Along with my race, my Catholicism has always been a pillar of my identity in this life, in this society. These two facets of my identity account for the way I think about, feel about, and react to almost everything that I experience and observe. And both were part of my upbringing from birth.

There is a room in my parents' house in Texas that I humorously took to calling several years ago "the colored museum." It is a veritable Wycliff family gallery. Photos cover almost every inch of wall space. The oldest picture, taken not many years after the Civil War, is of a woman ancestor three generations before my parents. The newest picture is also of a woman, a member of the third generation after my parents.

It says something important about our family that right along with the graduation photos and baby pictures and wedding and prom poses, my parents have hung the first communion class pictures of eight of their nine children, me and my seven younger siblings. The only one missing is the class picture of my older brother, Francois, and that's because, as best I can determine, it never existed. No picture was taken of him and his small class of first communicants at St. Joseph the Worker Church in Dayton, Texas.

The presence of those photos bespeaks the importance to my parents of their Catholic faith, and of our education and upbringing in it. But one particular aspect of those pictures makes that point with special force.

Take my picture, for example. It was shot on a sunny spring day in 1955, on the front steps of Holy Family Church in Ashland, Kentucky. There must have been at least fifty children in the class, girls and boys. But scan the faces and you'll see only one dark face among the first communicants: mine. The only other dark face in the photo is that of Francois, who, dressed in the cassock and surplice of an acolyte, stands to one side of the pastor, Monsignor Declan Carroll.

The other pictures show pretty much the same racial pattern, although there is at least a sprinkling of other African Americans in the classes of the youngest siblings. But when we washed up in Ashland, on the banks of the Ohio River east of Cincinnati, in autumn 1954, the Wycliffs were the only black family in the parish, and we children were the only black kids in the school.

You'd have had a hard time convincing me of it at first, but we were blessed to be there. Holy Family, I later realized, was for us an ark, a refuge. My father, who now is eighty-four, related to me a few years ago how we came to be on that ark. In one respect the story was very common to black people of that time; in another respect it was utterly uncommon.

Mother and Daddy both were born and raised in Dayton, a farming community in East Texas almost exactly halfway between Houston and Beaumont on U.S. Highway 90. Daddy was an only child; Mother was the second oldest of ten. Daddy's mother, my grandmother, was a Baptist; his father, my grandfather, was a Catholic. Daddy was raised "basically Baptist" and converted to Catholicism after he and Mother were married. Mother's parents both were Catholics, with roots in those Creole communities of southern Louisiana.

My parents, Wilbert and Emily, were married on June 2, 1942, in Bisbee, Arizona, where Daddy, an army lieutenant, was stationed at the time. Francois was born ten months later, in March 1943. Daddy shipped out to Italy with the all-black 92nd Division not long afterward.

After the war Daddy came home and, using his GI benefit, went part-time to the Texas State University for Negroes (now Texas Southern University) in Houston while working at various jobs to support his family. He earned his degree in industrial education in 1950. For his trouble he got a series of jobs that gave him inadequate pay and even less dignity. It would never be otherwise in the segregated South, he realized, and so he resolved to leave.

His ticket out was a civil-service exam that brought an offer of a job as an instructor of industrial arts at the Federal Correctional Institution—a federal prison—in Ashland,

Kentucky. He went there alone in June 1954 to see whether he and the job and the people in charge would all find one another agreeable. They did, and in August 1954 the family packed up and moved north to join him. By then, he and Mother had five children—Francois, me, Karen, Christopher, Ida—and a sixth, Joy, on the way.

Ashland was not exactly the racial promised land. In some respects it was worse than Dayton. We could not, for example, go to the downtown movie theaters at all in Ashland; we at least had been able to sit in the balcony in Dayton.

In one crucial respect, however, Ashland was an improvement: it had an alternative to the black public school, in the form of Holy Family School. Or at least it was a theoretical alternative, because to that date no black child had ever gone to the Catholic school.

Daddy recalled to me how he visited the black public school, Booker T. Washington, saw the decrepit building and equipment, and was heartsick at the thought of sending his children there. Part of the purpose of moving had been to get away from that sort of Jim Crow education.

It was his immediate supervisor at work, Walter Graybeal—a lapsed Catholic from Lafayette, Indiana; a white man who, Daddy swears, sacrificed his career advancement by routinely going to bat for Daddy—who first broached the idea of Holy Family as an alternative.

"You're a Catholic, aren't you, Wyc?" Graybeal asked. "Well, why shouldn't your kids go to the Catholic school?"

Why not? Daddy went to the parish and talked with Father Carroll. As he related it to me, the priest told him, "Well, Mr. Wycliff, I don't see why your children can't go to school here. But let me ask the bishop."

A day or so later, Daddy got a call at work. It was Father Carroll. "The bishop said the Catholic schools are for all

Catholic children," Father Carroll said. "Your children will be welcome here."

But that wasn't all of it. Father Carroll went the extra mile. On the Sunday before school was to start, he mounted the pulpit at Mass and laid down the law. One of Daddy's coworkers at the prison, Charles Eckenrode, who later became my confirmation sponsor, told him about it later. According to Eckenrode, Father Carroll announced that, starting that fall, there were going to be "colored children in our school. I want them treated properly. And anyone who doesn't will have to answer to me."

In those days, such words carried weight, coming from the Irish Catholic pastor of a largely Irish Catholic parish.

We were treated more than properly. I think it is fair to say that we were embraced as part of the Holy Family Parish family. To be sure, there was some nervousness at first. Mother tells of her anxiety in taking us to school on the first day—this was, after all, just months after the Supreme Court had overturned "separate but equal" public schooling in its now-celebrated *Brown* decision, and the South, of which Kentucky was definitely a part, was full of talk of "massive resistance."

But there was no such resistance at Holy Family. There was, Mother says, a moment's hesitation, and then another mother smiled, walked over to her, and introduced herself and her daughter, who was the same age and had the same name as my sister Karen. The ice was broken. "You'll never know what a smile can mean to a person," Mother says as she recalls that day.

I did not plan to be a journalist. I was going to be a teacher—a professor of political science. I graduated in June 1969 from the University of Notre Dame and was admitted to graduate study at the University of Chicago and given a fellowship to finance it.

It took me only a few weeks to realize that I did not want to be there. The University of Chicago was about as thoroughly disconnected from the neighborhood, the city, and the social ferment surrounding it as if it had been on the moon. And the lively engagement with people and ideas and social movements that I had enjoyed at Notre Dame was absent in the intense, isolated atmosphere of graduate school at Chicago.

Still, while I didn't want to be doing what I was where I was, I had no idea what else I might want or be able to do. Then came December 4, 1969.

I awoke just before 7:00 AM in my studio apartment at Forty-seventh Street and Drexel Boulevard and flipped on the radio next to my bed. The all-news stations crackled with word of a "shoot-out" overnight between units of the Chicago police assigned to the Cook County State's Attorney's Office and members of the Black Panther Party on the city's West Side. Two Panther leaders, Fred Hampton and Mark Clark, had been killed in the exchange.

I had no relationship to the Black Panthers. I knew Fred Hampton only by what I had seen of him during brief television interviews in the weeks preceding his death. But his words and his manner in those TV appearances suggested to me that this was no mere street thug. Indeed, I saw something of myself in Hampton: we were both young black men full of passion to see our people's lot improved. He was trying to do it one way; I was trying another. His got him killed—unjustly, I was convinced.

In the days and weeks following the "shoot-out," the Panther story consumed me. I would get up in the morning, buy every newspaper I could find, and devour the latest news. I watched every TV news show I could, and I listened to the radio constantly for news.

Gradually, the Chicago news media unearthed the truth. There had been no shoot-out; it had been a shoot-in by the police. Hampton and Clark had been deliberately targeted and slain.

As I watched the Chicago media do their splendid work, I began to feel attracted to that work as a socially relevant and useful way to spend a life. It was in every sense of the word a calling, a vocation.

It took until the end of the spring quarter at the University of Chicago for me to get up the gumption to strike out in a new direction. I packed up my books and my meager other belongings and headed home to Texas, to Houston.

I hoped to get into TV news, but—no surprise, really—I had no luck at the stations there. I finally made my way to the spanking-new offices of the *Houston Post* and filled out a job application, telling the lady in the personnel office that I wanted to be a reporter. I should have been surprised when they agreed to give me an interview—nobody walks into a big-city newspaper off the street and gets an interview, much less a job. But I suppose the educational pedigree helped. So did the fact that, at that time, there was all of one black reporter in the *Post* newsroom, and there was unease in the city over a Black Panther–type group that called itself People's Party II.

Anyway, I was interviewed and hired. The passion for justice and righteousness cultivated by my parents and teachers had led me to my profession.

I am blessed to have had a career of more than thirty years in the news industry. The last seventeen of those have been in the most rarefied part of the industry: opinion writing. I wrote editorials for more than five years at the *New York Times*. I did the same for ten years at the *Chicago Tribune,* and for nine of those years I served as editorial page editor. For the last two years, I have written a column of personal opinion, mainly about issues of media process and ethics but often about other matters as well.

The stock-in-trade of opinion writers is ideas—ideas that challenge, provoke, clarify. The Catholic Church, with possibly the oldest and richest intellectual history in the Western world, ought to be a powerful contender for the time and attention of columnists and editorial writers at the nation's newspapers. In my experience, however, it is not. The reasons are complex.

There is an enormous amount of anti-Catholic sentiment in newsrooms, as there is in society at large. Some of it is plain old lowbrow bigotry—I've heard Catholics referred to on more than one occasion as "mackerel snappers." Some is more sophisticated, such as holding the pope responsible for famine and starvation because of the church's official opposition to artificial birth control and abortion. And some is rooted in the conviction, not entirely unjustified, that the church has over the centuries fostered or tolerated anti-Semitism and other assorted kinds of bigotry and intolerance, and therefore is not to be trusted.

But the antagonistic attitudes of others are nothing compared to the wounds the church has inflicted upon itself. It will be decades before the anguish and the anger generated by the clergy sex abuse scandals dissipate, before innocent mentions of priestly concern and care don't provoke snickering, before the church enjoys the sort of regard it once took for granted. And this is a totally self-inflicted injury.

On top of this, Catholicism suffers from the same thing in attempting to influence the news media as it does in its pulpits on Sunday mornings: bad preaching. The church simply does not have many spokesmen—any spokesmen?—who can speak its message in ways that make it relevant and understandable to modern men and women of a secularist bent. Add to this the fact that the church's message is fundamentally a counter-cultural one, and thus a demanding one, and the problem of making the message understood is compounded.

Additionally—and this will not be much appreciated by Catholic liberals—the Catholic Church in America has become a Tower of Babel. Non-Catholics—and many Catholics as well—have become confused because there is no Catholic trademark to distinguish a so-called Catholic opinion from another. The brand name "Catholic" has been devalued in the marketplace through confusion. Catholics for a Free Choice is the same as any other Catholic group of opinion—or at least that's what the Catholic professor on CNN or ABC or in the *New York Times* said.

For a Catholic like me, attempting to bring what little I know of the distinguished Catholic intellectual tradition to bear on deliberations in the newsroom or the editorial boardroom, this causes fits. Not only am I unable to speak authoritatively about Catholic positions, but I am unable to *feel* authoritatively as well.

So what do I do? I try to go with the basics. I read a lot of Scripture and try to apply what I read to the situations that present themselves in the news. Interestingly, the older I get, the more I find myself attracted to the passages about forgiveness and reconciliation. I suspect that's not coincidental.

But always, always, the most powerful passage of all is about Judgment Day, Matthew 25:31–46, especially verse 40: "I assure you, as often as you did it for one of my least brothers, you did it for me."

Hep! Hep! Hep!

Cynthia Ozick

from *Portland Magazine*

Editor's note: Some readers may wonder why exactly a searing essay about anti-Semitism and hatred for the Jews and the brave and savage histories of Israel and Palestine is featured in a collection of "Catholic writing." Answer: Judaism is the seed from which we grew, the faith of Jesus and all his friends and family and followers, and what happens to the people to whom I Am Who Am spoke directly is of pressing concern today to Christians of every stripe. What Ozick has to say about the cold return of an ancient evil should be pretty much required reading for every Catholic man, woman, and child.

We thought it was finished. The ovens are long cooled, the anti-vermin gas dissipated into purifying clouds, cleansed air, nightmarish fable. The cries of the naked, decades gone, are mute; the bullets splitting throats and breasts and skulls, the human waterfall of bodies tipping over into the wooded ravine at Babi Yar, are no more than tedious footnotes on aging paper. The deportation ledgers, with their scrupulous lists of names of the doomed—what are they now? Museum artifacts.

The heaps of eyeglasses and children's shoes, the hills of human hair, lie disintegrating in their display cases, while only a little distance away the visitors' cafeteria bustles and buzzes: sandwiches, Cokes, the waiting tour buses.

We thought it was finished. In the middle of the twentieth century, and surely by the end of it, we thought it was finished, genuinely finished, the bloodlust finally slaked. We thought it was finished, that heads were hanging—the heads of the leaders and schemers on gallows, the heads of the bystanders and onlookers in shame. The Topf company, manufacturer of the ovens, went belatedly out of business, belatedly disgraced and shamed. Out of shame German publishers of Nazi materials concealed and falsified the past. Out of shame Paul de Man, lauded and eminent Yale intellectual, concealed his early Nazi lucubrations. Out of shame Mircea Eliade, lauded and eminent Chicago intellectual, concealed his membership in Romania's Nazi-linked Iron Guard. Out of shame memorials to the murdered rose up. Out of shame synagogues were rebuilt in the ruins of November 9, 1938, the night of fire and pogrom and the smashing of windows. Out of shame those who were hounded like prey and fled for their lives were invited back to their native villages and towns and cities, to be celebrated as successful escapees from the murderous houndings of their native villages and towns and cities. Shame is salubrious: it acknowledges inhumanity, it admits to complicity, it induces remorse. Naively, foolishly, stupidly, hopefully, ahistorically, we thought that shame and remorse—worldwide shame, worldwide remorse—would endure. Naively, foolishly, stupidly, hopefully, ahistorically, we thought that the cannibal hatred, once quenched, would not soon wake again.

It has awakened.

In "The Modern Hep! Hep! Hep!"—an 1878 essay reflecting on the condition of the Jews—George Eliot noted that it would be "difficult to find a form of bad reasoning about [Jews] which had not been heard in conversation or been admitted to the dignity of print." She was writing in a period politically not unlike our own—Disraeli ascendant in England, Jews prominent in liberal parties both in Germany and France. Yet her title points to something far deadlier than mere "bad reasoning." "Hep!" was the cry of the crusaders as they swept through Europe, annihilating one Jewish community after another; it stood for *Hierosolyma est perdita* (Jerusalem is destroyed) and was taken up again by anti-Jewish rioters in Germany in 1819. In this single raging syllable, past and future met, and in her blunt bold enunciation of it, George Eliot was joining bad reasoning—i.e., canard and vilification—to its consequences: violence and murder. The Jews, she wrote, have been "regarded and treated very much as beasts hunted for their skins," and the curse on them, the charge of deicide, was counted a justification for hindering them from pursuing agriculture and handicraft; for marking them out as execrable figures by a peculiar dress; for torturing them, spitting at them, and pelting them; for taking it for certain that they killed and ate babies, poisoned the wells, and took pains to spread the plague; for putting it to them whether they would be baptized or burned, and not failing to burn and massacre them when they were obstinate, but also for suspecting them of disliking their baptism when they had got it, and then burning them in punishment of their insincerity; finally, for hounding them by tens on tens of thousands from their homes, where they had found shelter for centuries, and inflicting on them the horrors of a new exile and a new dispersion. All of this to avenge the Savior of humankind, or else to compel these stiff-necked people to acknowledge a Master whose servants showed such beneficent effects of his teaching.

As an anti-Semitic yelp, "Hep!" is long out of fashion. In the eleventh century it was already a substitution and a metaphor:

Jerusalem meant Jews, and "Jerusalem is destroyed" was, when knighthood was in flower, an incitement to pogrom. Today, the modern "Hep!" appears in the form of Zionism, Israel, Sharon. And the connection between vilification and the will to undermine and endanger Jewish lives is as vigorous as when the howl of "Hep!" was new. The French ambassador to Britain, his tongue unbuttoned in a London salon, hardly thinks to cry "Hep!"; instead, he speaks of "that shitty little country." European and British scholars and academicians, their Latin gone dry, will never cry "Hep!"; instead, they call for the boycott of Israeli scholars and academicians.

Nearly all of this had precedent in the church Luther renounced, and even the medieval church practiced mimicry. It was Pope Innocent III who implemented the yellow badge of ignominy (Hitler was no innovator, except as to gas chambers)—yet Innocent too was innocent of originality, since he took the idea from Prince Abu-Yusef Almansur, a Moroccan Muslim ruler of the thirteenth century. Post-Enlightenment France may be known for its merciless persecution of a guiltless Dreyfus, and for the anti-Jewish rioting it set off, and, more recently, for the gendarmes who arrested and deported the Jews of Paris with a zeal equal to that of the Germans. But Paris had seen anti-Jewish mobs before—for instance, in June of 1242, when twenty-four cartloads of Talmuds were set afire in a public square. And while elsewhere in France, and all through the Rhineland, the crusaders were busy at their massacres, across the Channel the archbishop of Canterbury was issuing a decree designed to prevent the Jews of England from having access to food.

All of this, let it be noted, preceded the barbarities of the Inquisition: the scourgings, the burnings, the confiscations, the expulsions. Any attempt to set down the record, early and late, of Christian violence against Jews can only be a kind of pointillism—an atrocity here, another there, and again another. The nineteenth-century historian Heinrich Graetz (as rationalist in temperament as Gibbon) summed up the predicament of Jews across the whole face of Europe: if Jewish history were to follow chronicles, memorial books, and martyrologies, its pages would be filled with bloodshed, it would consist of horrible exhibitions of corpses, and it would stand forth to make accusation against a doctrine that taught princes and nations to become common executioners and hangmen. For, from the thirteenth century to the sixteenth, the persecutions and massacres of the Jews increased with frightful rapidity and intensity and only alternated with inhuman decrees issued by both church and the state, the aim and purport of all of which were to humiliate the Jews, to brand them with calumny, and to drive them to suicide . . . The nations of Europe emulated one another in exercising their cruelty upon the Jews . . . In Germany they were slain by the thousands . . . Every year martyrs fell, now in Weissenburg, Magdeburg, Arnstadt; now in Coblenz, Sinzig, Erfurt, and other places. In Sinzig all the members of the congregation were burned alive on a Sabbath in their synagogue. There were German Christian families who boasted that they had burned Jews, and in their pride assumed the name of Judenbrater (Jew-roaster).

And all of this, let it again be noted, before the Shoah; before the czarist pogroms and the czarist fabrication of "The Protocols of the Elders of Zion"; before the exclusions, arrests, and Gulag brutalities of the Soviet Union; before the shooting of the Soviet Yiddish writers in the basement of Moscow's Lubyanka prison; before the rise of contemporary Islamist demonization of Jews; before the eight-decades-long Arab assault on Jewish national aspiration and sovereignty; before the Palestinian cult of suicide bombing. Anti-Semitism feeds on itself from continent to continent, from Iceland to Japan; it scarcely requires living Jews. Its source is commonly taken to be the two supersessionist Scriptures that derive from Judaism—in Christianity, the Jews' cry (in the Gospel of Matthew) of "His blood be on us and on our children," the fount of the venomous deicide curse; in Islam, the unwillingness of Jews to follow Muhammad in the furtherance of a latter-day faith, which accused the Hebrew Bible of distorting the biblical narratives that appear, Islam claims, more authoritatively and genuinely in the Koran.

But anti-Semitism originated in neither Christianity nor Islam. It first burst out in Egypt, in the third century BCE, during the reign of Ptolemy II, when Manetho, an Egyptian priest, in a polemic directed against the biblical account in Genesis and Exodus, described a people who "came from Jerusalem" as the descendants of a mob of lepers. Against the Hebrew text, which records Joseph as a wise and visionary governor, Manetho charged that Joseph defiled the shrines and statues of the gods and set fire to villages and towns. Nor did Moses liberate the Hebrews and bring them, under divine guidance, out of Egypt, from slavery to freedom. These offspring of lepers, Manetho declared, were ignominiously expelled, having savagely despoiled the country for thirteen years. Such calumnies soon infiltrated Hellenic literature. The Greeks, detecting no plastic representation of the divine order, were quick to name the Jews atheists—lazy atheists, since once in seven days they refrained from labor. The Greek scholar Mnaseas of Patara recycled an Egyptian myth (traces of it later turned up in Plutarch) that asserted that the temple in Jerusalem harbored the golden head of an ass, the sole object of the Jews' worship. Another version had the Jews praying before an image of Moses seated on an ass while displaying a book containing laws of hatred for all humanity.

Greek enmity was most acutely encapsulated in the canard spread by Apion, whose contribution to the history of anti-Semitism is the infamously enduring blood libel. In its earliest form, a Greek, captured by Jews, is taken to the temple, fattened, and then killed; his entrails are ritually eaten in conjunction with an oath of hatred toward Greeks. Christian mythology altered the Greek to a Christian, usually a child, whose blood was said to be drained at Passover for the purpose of being baked into matzah. From its Christian source, the blood libel leached into Muslim societies. It surfaced most recently in a Saudi newspaper, which fantasized Muslim blood in Purim cakes. Mustafa Tlas, the Syrian defense minister, is the author of *The Matzah of Zion,* which presents the 1841 Damascus blood libel as an established "Jewish ritual." And in a writing contest sponsored by the Palestinian Ministry of Education, the winning entry, by a tenth grader, described a Mother's Day gift an Israeli soldier brings to his mother: "a bottle of the blood of a Palestinian child he has murdered."

Current anti-Semitism, accelerating throughout advanced and sophisticated Europe—albeit under the rubric of anti-Zionism, and masked by the deceptive lingo of human rights—purports to eschew such primitivism. After all, Nazism and Stalinism are universally condemned; anti-Judaism is seen as obscurantist medievalism; the Vatican's theology of deicide was nullified four decades ago; Lutherans, at least in America, vigorously dissociate themselves from their founder's execrations of the Jews; and whatever the vestiges of Europe's unregenerate (and often Holocaust-denying) Right may think, its vociferous Left would no more depart from deploring the Holocaust than it would be willing to be deprived of its zeal in calumniating the Jewish state. It is easy enough to shed a tear or two for the shed and slandered blood of the Jews of the past; no one will praise Torquemada, or honor Goebbels.

But to stand up for truth telling in the present, in a mythologizing atmosphere of pervasive defamation and fabrication, is not a job for cowards.

In the time of Goebbels, the Big Lie about the Jews was mainly confined to Germany alone; much of the rest of the world saw through it with honest clarity. In our time, the Big Lie (or Big Lies, there are so many) is disseminated everywhere, and not merely by the ignorant, but with malice aforethought by the intellectual classes, the governing elites, the most prestigious elements of the press in all the capitals of Europe, and by the university professors and the diplomats.

The contemporary Big Lie, of course, concerns the Jews of Israel: they are oppressors in the style of the Nazis; they ruthlessly pursue, and perpetuate, "occupation" solely for the sake of domination and humiliation; they purposefully kill Palestinian children; their military have committed massacres; their government "violates international law"; their nationhood and their sovereignty have no legitimacy; they are intruders and usurpers inhabiting an illicit "entity," and not a people entitled as other peoples are entitled; and so on and so on. Reviving both blood libel and deicide, respectable European journals publish political cartoons showing Prime Minister Sharon devouring Palestinian babies, and Israeli soldiers bayoneting the infant Jesus.

Yet the modern history of Jews in the Holy Land overwhelmingly refutes these scurrilities. It is the Arabs, not the Jews, who have been determined to dispose of a people's right to live in peace. Is there any point now—after so many politically willed erasures of fact by Palestinian Arabs, Muslim populations in general, and a mean-spirited European intelligentsia—to recapitulate the long record of Arab hostility that has prevailed since the demise of the Ottoman Empire? The Muslim Arab claim of hegemony (through divine fiat, possessive greed, contempt for pluralism, or all three) over an entire region of the globe accounts for the hundreds of Christian Arabs who have fled Bethlehem, Nablus, Ramallah, and all other places where

Muslims dominate—a flight rarely reported. Unsurprisingly, the Christians who have not yet departed blame the Israelis for this displacement, not the Muslim extremists under whose threats of reprisal they live. As for the fate of Jews in the orbit of this self-declared Muslim imperium, the current roar of "resistance to occupation" is notoriously belied by the bloody Arab pogroms of 1920, 1921, 1929, 1936, and 1939, when there was no Jewish state at all, let alone any issue of "settlements." The 1929 attacks left Hebron, the site of an ancient and uninterrupted Jewish community, effectively *Judenrein*.

What use is there, in the face of brute political and cultural intransigence, in rehearsing the events of 1948? In that year Arab rejection of an independent Palestinian state under the UN partition plan led to the invasion by five Arab armies intent on crushing nascent Jewish sovereignty; whole sections of Jerusalem were destroyed or overrun. The year 1948 marked the second, though not the last, Arab refusal of Palestinian statehood. The first came in 1937, when under the British mandate the Peel Commission proposed partition and statehood for the Arabs of Palestine; the last occurred in 2000, when Arafat dismissed statehood in favor of a well-prepared and programmatic violence. (The flouting of the road map by Palestinian unwillingness to dismantle terror gangs will have counted as the Palestinians' fourth refusal of statehood, but the road map's callously criminalizing equation of civilian inhabitants of Jewish towns—settlements—with Palestinian murder of Jewish civilians is itself egregious.) After 1948, the Arab war against the Jews of Israel continued through the terror incursions of 1956, the Six-Day War of 1967, the Yom Kippur attacks of 1973, and the fomented violence of 1987, the so-called first intifada.

In short, for two-thirds of a century the Arabs have warred against a Jewish presence in "their" part of the world. The 1967 war in defense of Jewish lives (when affected Jews everywhere went into mourning, fearing catastrophe) culminated in Golda Meir's attempt to return, in exchange for peace, the territories that, in the spirit of partition, Israel had never sought to acquire, and had so unexpectedly conquered. The answer came at an Arab summit in Khartoum: no negotiations, no recognition, no peace. So much for the "crime" of occupation.

And though the Oslo Accords of 1993 strove yet again for negotiations, most energetically under Ehud Barak, both the Palestinian leadership and the Palestinian public chose killing over compromise—this time with newly conceived atrocities through suicide bombings, always directed against civilians, in buses, cafés, restaurants, supermarkets, or wherever Israelis peacefully congregate.

This is the history that is ignored or denigrated or distorted or spitefully misrepresented. And because it is a history that has been assaulted and undermined by worldwide falsehoods in the mouths of pundits and journalists, in Europe and all over the Muslim world, the distinction between anti-Semitism and anti-Zionism has finally and utterly collapsed. It is only sophistry, disingenuousness, and corrupted conscience that continue to insist on such a distinction. To fail to trace the pernicious consistencies of Arab political aims from 1920 until today, despite temporary pretensions otherwise, is to elevate intellectual negligence to a principle. To transmogrify self-defense into aggression is to invite an Orwellian horselaugh. To identify occupation as Israel's primal sin—the most up-to-date "Hep!" of all—is to be blind to Arab actions and intentions before 1967, and to be equally blind to Israel's repeated commitments to negotiated compromise. On the Palestinian side, the desire to eradicate Jewish nationhood increases daily: it is as if 1948 has returned, replicated in the guise of fanatical young "martyrs" systematically indoctrinated in kindergartens and schools and camps—concerning whom it is cant to say, as many do, that they strap detonators to their loins because they are without hope. It is hope that inflames them.

Perhaps the most bizarre display of international anti-Semitism was flaunted at Durban, during a UN conference ostensibly called to condemn "racism, racial discrimination, xenophobia, and related intolerance." Plucked from the refuse heap, the old UN canard "Zionism is racism," together with a determined Arab hijacking of the agenda, brought about the bitterest irony of all: a virulent hatred under the auspices of anti-hatred. At Durban the Jewish state was declared to have been conceived in infamy, Jewish representatives were threatened, and language was violated more savagely than at any time since the Nazi era. "Political language," said Orwell, "is designed to make lies sound truthful and murder respectable, and to give the appearance of solidity to pure wind." Yet the rant that emerged at Durban—those instantly recognizable snarls of anti-Semitism—hardly merited the term *political*. It had the venerable sound of the mob: Hep! Hep! Hep!

Anti-Semitism is a foolish word; we appear to be stuck with it. *Semitism* has virtually no meaning. The Semites are a linguistic group encompassing Hebrew, Akkadian, Amharic, and Arabic. *Anti-Semitism* (a term fabricated a century ago by a euphemistic German anti-Semite) signifies hatred of Jews, and hatred's easy corollary: a steady drive to weaken, to hurt, and to extirpate Jews.

Still, one must ask: Why the Jews? A sad old joke pluckily confronts the enigma:

—The Jews and the bicyclists are at the bottom of all the world's ills.

—Why the bicyclists?

—Why the Jews?

. . . which implies that blaming one set of irrelevancies is just as irrational as blaming the other. Ah, but it is never the bicyclists, and it is always the Jews.

There are innumerable social, economic, and political speculations as to cause: scapegoatism, envy, exclusionary practices, the temptation of a demographic majority to subjugate a demographic minority, the attempt by corrupt rulers to deflect attention from the failings of their tyrannical regimes, and more.

But any of these can burst out in any society against any people—so why always the Jews? A metaphysical explanation is proffered: the forceful popular resistance to what Jewish civilization represents—the standard of ethical monotheism and its demands on personal and social conscience. Or else it is proposed, in Freudian terms, that Christianity and Islam, each in its turn, sought to undo the parent religion, which was seen as an authoritative rival it was needful to surpass and displace.

This last notion, however, has no standing in contemporary Christianity. In nearly all Christian communities, there is remorse for the old theologically instigated crimes, as well as serious internal moral restitution, much of it of a very high order. But a salient fact remains, perhaps impolitic to note: relief has come through Christianity's having long been depleted of temporal power. Today's Islamists, by contrast, are supported and succored by states: Iran, Syria (and Lebanon, its vassal), Saudi Arabia, Sudan, Libya, Malaysia, Indonesia, Pakistan, Egypt (which suppresses its domestic extremists, while its official press, film industry, and other institutions encourage anti-Zionist incitements). Iranian weapons flood into Gaza, whether by sea or through tunnels from Egypt. Saudi Arabia not long ago unashamedly broadcast a telethon to collect millions to be sent to Palestinian terror gangs; it continues today as Hamas's chief funder. And though Saddam Hussein is finally gone, it will not be forgotten that he honored and enriched the families of suicide bombers. (I observe a telltale omission: those who deny any linkage between Iraq and terror universally discount Saddam's lavish payments to Hamas and Islamic Jihad.)

But if one cannot account for the tenacity of anti-Semitism, one can readily identify it. It wears its chic disguises. It breeds on the tongues of liars. The lies may be noisy and primitive and preposterous, like the widespread Islamist charge (doggerelized by New Jersey's poet laureate) that a Jewish conspiracy leveled the Twin Towers. Or the lies may take the form of skilled patter in a respectable timbre, while retailing sleight-of-hand trickeries—such as the hallucinatory notion that the defensive measures of a perennially beleaguered people constitute colonization and victimization, or that the Jewish state is to blame for the aggressions committed against it. Lies shoot up from the rioters in Gaza and Ramallah. Insinuations ripple out of the high tables of Oxbridge. And steadily, whether from the street or the salon, one hears the enduring old cry: "Hep! Hep! Hep!"

As I write, fresh news arrives—evidence of the fulfillment of one martyr's hope. An Israeli doctor and his twenty-year-old daughter have this day been blown up together in a café, where they had gone for a father-daughter talk on the eve of the young woman's marriage. She had been devoting her year of national service to the care of children with cancer; her ambition was to study medicine for the sake of such children. Her father was an eminent and remarkable physician, the tireless head of a hospital emergency room that tends the victims of terror attacks. He had just returned from the United States, where he was instructing American doctors in the lifesaving emergency techniques he had pioneered. Father and daughter were buried on what was to have been the daughter's wedding day.

The Threat of Same-Sex Marriage

Robert Sokolowski

from *America*

Those who argue *against* the legalization of same-sex marriages insist that marriage is ordered toward the procreation of children and that the legal supports given to marriage are given with that end in view. Marriage needs the protection of laws because society must be concerned about its preservation and continuity into the next generation.

Those who argue *for* legalization claim that an abiding friendship between two persons should be acknowledged by law, and the legal benefits accruing to marriage should be made available to the partners. As a recent letter in the *Wall Street Journal* stated, "Marriage is a personal decision of commitment and love, and should be as open to homosexuals as it is to heterosexuals." The essential point in the argument for legalization is that marriage as an institution sanctions a friendship, not specifically a procreative relationship.

Defenders of same-sex marriages often ask their opponents what they fear. What damage will follow from legally recognizing same-sex unions? How will such recognition threaten heterosexual marriages?

Well, here are some of the consequences of giving same-sex marriages full legal status.

Suppose our laws were to recognize homosexual marriages. Then suppose I were to come along and say: "My uncle and I [or my aunt and I, or my sister and I, or my mother and I, or my father and I, or my friend and I] live together. We are devoted to each other, but we don't engage in mutual sexual conduct. We want to get married in order to get the legal benefits of marriage that affect property rights, taxes, insurance, and the like."

The reply would probably be negative, at least at first. The laws would say, "You cannot get married." Why not? "Because you don't exchange sex." That is, the homosexual marriage would become the paradigm. The exchange of sex, and specifically nonprocreative sex, would be what defines marriage. This new definition of marriage would be implied by the refusal to let my uncle and me get married, not because we cannot have children but because we do not choose to have sex. A procreative marriage would then only accidentally be a marriage. Procreation would no longer specify what a marriage is.

Once this new definition of marriage is in place, subsequent laws would have to shore it up. What effect would this development have on the public sense of family and marriage? What effect would it have on sex education? It should also be noted that this understanding of marriage would bring the government into the bedroom with a vengeance, because it would be necessary for it to verify that those who are married are indeed having sex.

But suppose the reply of the laws to my demand to marry my uncle or aunt is "All right, we will declare you married. We have already separated marriage from reproduction, and from now on we will separate marriage from sex entirely. Any two people who live together can get married." After all, if homosexual couples aren't discriminated against according to the new definition of marriage, why should any two people who live together, even those already related by prior "familial" bonds, such as uncles and nephews, be discriminated against? Any persons who form a household should have the right to be married.

What effect would this have on the sense of marriage? I could marry my father (even Oedipus was never in danger of doing this, so far have we surpassed the wisdom of the ancients). I could marry someone I plan to live with for a few years, just for the benefit of it all. Suppose I were to move in with my grandfather who is seriously ill, to help him out in his last days. We could get married for the legal benefits and to facilitate the inheritance.

And once this has been done, why not permit polygamy and polyandry? Why discriminate against groups, if just living together is the only requirement for marriage? I could marry not just my mother or my father but both of them together, in a truly deconstructionist gesture, thus joining not with one but with both of the sources of my being.

We could even go one step further and ask why people should have to live together to be married. If there are legal and financial benefits to the union, why should they not be available to any people who wish to take advantage of them? The choice to be benefited should override the accidentality of living together, so long as there is a modicum of commitment and friendship between those people.

If "marriage is a personal decision of commitment and love," why should it not be open to whoever is (or says he or she is) committed to and loves anyone else to a greater or lesser degree, whether singly or in a collective? And why must that love be erotic? The major threat that same-sex marriages pose to traditional unions is that they redefine the institution of marriage.

Sexuality has as its end the procreation of children, but the common use of contraception and the way sex is presented in our popular culture have totally separated sex from procreation in public opinion. Sex is understood as an end in itself. The reigning opinion is that a woman gets pregnant by accident, by not taking precautions, not because sexual activity is procreative and its natural outcome is conception. This is a great reversal of nature and accident. Furthermore, it is said that every child must be a wanted child, which implies that the child is loved because the child has been chosen, not because he or she is there.

It is often said that we have recently arrived at a new and different sense of sexuality and marriage, but this claim is incorrect; both are what they always were. To say that mutual love is on a par with procreation as an end in marriage is misleading. It is obviously very important, but not as a simply parallel good. Rather, the end of procreation is what specifies this relationship; the physical end of procreation is the first and essential defining character of marriage, and sex is defined as the power to procreate. Then this relationship, so defined, is to be informed with friendship or love—that is, mutual benevolence—but the kind of love it calls for is qualified by the type of relationship it is.

Even in the Catholic Church after the Second Vatican Council, people have been quick to introduce mutual love as an end of marriage on a par with procreation. It is, of course, an end of marriage, but not the same kind of end as procreation is. It is not an alternative end, but one based on and specified by the procreative relationship.

People who separate sexuality from procreation, whether in their thinking or their actions, live in illusion. They lie about this matter, to themselves and others. Furthermore, this error occurs not about some marginal human thing, but about the mystery of our origins. It is an illusion concerning one of the most powerful human emotions and tendencies. Once we live in delusion about such an important issue, we will inevitably be misguided in regard to many other human things: religion, human relations, laws, governmental policies, moral judgments, and even our cultural inheritance. The most obvious truths become obscured.

The state does not establish legal categories for many different forms of human friendship. Why does it do so for marriage? Because it has an interest in society's next generation. The continuation of the population is a condition for the survival of the body politic. It is this focus on population and reproduction that justifies laws concerning marriage. Even marriages between people who cannot have children, such as older people, depend on procreative marriages for their sense and legal standing. Society has an interest in seeing that there will be a next generation and that it will be brought up to be virtuous, law-abiding, and productive. By its actions, therefore, the state has traditionally recognized reproduction as the end of marriage.

Proponents of same-sex marriages want to unlink marriage from reproduction and have the laws legalize their friendship because it is a friendship, not because it is procreative. But once the state legalizes one kind of friendship, it cannot stop at that; it will have to legalize any and all friendships for which legalization is sought.

The concept of same-sex marriage leads to impossibilities, because it contains a contradiction. Its proponents do not recognize the contradiction, because they think that nothing has a natural end, and specifically they think that marriage and sexuality do not have natural ends. They think that choices and purposes are the only things that matter, and that the private choices they make, their "personal decisions of commitment and love," must be ratified and supported by public law.

I Am the Church

Alice L. Camille and Joel Schorn

from *U.S. Catholic*

Claire didn't think of herself as Catholic, quite frankly, until she was in her forties. She had been raised by Catholic parents and baptized as a baby, and she had even attended parochial schools for a while. But she decided early on that the "Catholic experiment" had proved unsuccessful. She spent most of her school years in trouble, and the Sunday church scene seemed byzantine. The Catholic identity just didn't stick to her life in any meaningful way, or so it seemed at the time. When she stopped going to church, her parents didn't object, and by the time she was out on her own, she had forgotten about the church altogether.

One failed marriage, a reluctant abortion, and three decades later, Claire was about as far from the church as she could imagine being. Still, she found herself standing in a Catholic church again, waiting to speak to a priest. Her father had died, her mother was too distraught to take care of the arrangements, and Claire knew it was her father's wish to be buried with a Catholic funeral. Though at this time in her life Claire was the successful owner of her own business, the idea of talking to a priest made her feel about twelve years old and oddly scared.

But nothing happened the way she had anticipated. The priest was young and gentle-spoken, not like the grouchy old pastor locked in her childhood memory. The young priest was very sympathetic to her story, and this was so unexpected that she found herself crying and talking for the next hour about the struggles of her life—things she certainly hadn't planned on saying, and to a priest of all people!

He asked her if she intended this to be a matter for confession; not really understanding what he meant, she nodded, and he gave her absolution. Though Claire had often had regrets about the turns her life had taken, it had never occurred to her that there could be forgiveness, an end to the remorse and the responsibility, a way to find healing and start over. Despite the pain of her present mission, Claire found herself glad and grateful to be standing in that church.

The funeral for her father later that week was a moving and powerful experience. She took communion at the funeral for the first time as an adult, and suddenly this action, which had always seemed meaningless, became significant and comforting in a way that echoed through her for days afterward. Without intending to, without even consciously choosing to, Claire found herself belonging in that place again and wanting to be there.

As incredible as it still seems to her a decade later, Claire returned to the church, body and soul, that winter. She even received training to become a eucharistic minister and to extend that opportunity of belonging to others. "Being Catholic is the bottom line for me now," she admits with great enthusiasm. "I didn't just come back to the church—I am the church. I won't give up my seat again."

Claire is just one of the legion of Catholics who find themselves on the outside of the church for years and then make their way back. A majority of Catholics who abdicate their seat in the church do return at some point in their lives, and the routes back are as varied as the reasons they left. Some come back to raise their children with a strong set of values. Others feel a void that could not be filled by relationships and creature comforts. Some report a specific spiritual need or a lack of meaning that drew them back. Those who come from families with close ties to the church may eventually feel remorse about being away from the sacraments. Certain life events may precipitate a second look at the church: a family crisis or a marriage breakdown, a move to a new community, even an explicitly religious experience.

Catholics who return cite certain factors as very inviting. Parishes that exhibit a participatory style of leadership are attractive, as are those that offer varied worship experiences and programs aimed at the returnee's particular age group or life experience. Nothing beats a direct encounter with a warm and sympathetic representative of the church, such as the one Claire had. Parishes that advertise in the bulletin or local newspaper that they welcome Catholics who have been away and have a support group for returnees are likely to get returning Catholics.

Ray came back to the church through such a group at age thirty. From the time he knew he was gay, in his teens, being Catholic no longer seemed an option. His life took a dramatically new trajectory, away from his hometown, the confused response of his family members, and the religion that had always seemed to say "negative things about sex in general—and double that if you're homosexual." Ray moved to a gay-friendly city and found support for the person he understood himself to be in a strong community and life-giving relationships. It was painful to look back, so he tried to keep his focus on the present and the future.

"Then the future got shaky," he says simply. "Friends got sick, people got scared, my family wasn't there for me. Yet God had always been there, as strange as that may seem. I never doubted God, and I always had a reliance on the sense of the sacred. I even used to light candles for friends in trouble, that sort of thing. I knew I wasn't alone, that ultimately there was love and acceptance."

Ray may not have returned to the church, however, if it hadn't been for the ad he saw in the Sunday newspaper: "It was this outrageous photo of Lucille Ball tasting something awful and making such a grimace! The headline read, 'Catholicism leave a bad taste in your mouth? Come and talk about it!' I had to laugh. I thought, 'These people can laugh at themselves. That's a good sign.'"

Ray attended the advertised meeting at that church. He found a group of Catholics both in and out of the church who listened without judgment, asked sympathetic questions, and invited each person to come to Mass that Sunday and sit in the pews together. When he showed up that week, Ray was surprised how many others from the group did too. Afterward they went out for coffee and agreed they were more than a little homesick for the church. They decided to keep coming back to the parish-sponsored meetings and to Mass. With a little support they began to think they could work out their differences.

Ray came back to the church because of an explicit invitation. In Paul's case, no invitation was necessary for him to return—unless you count the hunger for God an invitation. He had exited the church in his teens and stayed away for fifteen years. Today he is a priest. When asked about the specifics of his departure, he says: "Two things made me stop going to church. The first was that I began to see a real gap between what the priests preached and how they lived. It seemed that all the money that the church collected for charity just got pumped back into the church facility. I didn't see the church helping the poor; it just seemed like they were helping themselves.

"The second thing was a growing disbelief that condemnation could be so universal. Based on what I was hearing, just about everybody was going to hell. But I really didn't think God would damn someone for eating a hot dog on a Friday. So the whole thing began to fall apart for me, and as I gained more freedom from my parents, I stopped going."

Paul admits he still struggles with some of the issues that drove him away as a kid: "The harsh conservatism of many church leaders still tends to discourage people. Also, the church still seems to spend much of its time, energy, and resources protecting the institution and guarding its entrances. It seems to me that the church sets up unnecessary obstacles that block the way of people seeking to move closer to God.

"I remain Catholic for the same reason I returned: I think I can make a difference. I believe God is calling me to be part of the force that is reforming the church and bringing it closer to what it's supposed to be."

For those just emerging into adulthood with newfound independence and personal power, it can be an overwhelming challenge to remain faithful to the simpler spiritual values learned in the family circle. Yet many do. How do they do it, and why?

"My parents aren't what I would have called 'real religious,'" Amy confesses. "They took us to Mass on Sundays, and we prayed before meals and at bedtime when we were little.

But we didn't talk about our faith or anything like that. It was just understood, like the cross hanging in the living room and the small sculpture of the Last Supper in the kitchen. They didn't make a big deal out of it, but in the background of every decision they made for us was this fidelity, to God and to love. Without a lot of pious drama, that was it."

In college many of Amy's friends tried alternative spiritual paths. Amy dutifully went with her crowd to try meditation at the local Vedanta center or to hear lectures on Buddhism or transcendental meditation. But she always came back convinced she'd had the same experiences and heard the same message before—at the Newman Center, where she attended the weekly folk Mass and signed up for an occasional half hour of adoration before the Blessed Sacrament. "Maybe it was less cool to do all this in church instead of with the swamis, but I had to admit it all pointed to the same thing," she says.

Today Amy has her own apartment, and on the wall of her bedroom is a small cross. In the main room is a portrait of Our Lady of Guadalupe. "These are just signs of something deeper about who I am," she says. "Being Catholic is not something I need to advertise, but it's the grass I walk on. I hope it will keep me true, the way it kept my parents."

Megan's experience of growing up Catholic was a little different. "My parents were social-justice hippies," she says. "I remember losing a baby tooth while picketing a lab where bombs were made. And I protested racial injustice before I understood what it meant. My folks always equated being Catholic with being part of 'the cause.' It never occurred to me that you could just go to Mass on Sunday and be done with it."

This unusual childhood experience seemed very normal at the time. "OK, I admit I came home a few times wanting something the other kids were talking about at school, like three hours of junk TV a night or Guess jeans. Sometimes I didn't really want to hear about the greenhouse effect; I just wanted to know why we couldn't have a bigger family car! But Mom wasn't rigid about this stuff. She'd explain to me about kids my age working in sweatshops and then tell me I could have any pair of jeans I wanted during back-to-school shopping. And in the end, I just couldn't let her buy the designer pants. I just couldn't be that big of a jerk."

Amy and Megan both think of themselves as "lifer" Catholics, in it for the long haul because of the steadfast influence that religious faith had on their parents. They appreciate the values they were taught and seek to emulate them. They believe that staying close to the church will get them where they hope to go as faithful adults.

David's relationship with the church has not been as uniformly smooth as Amy's or Megan's, and he admits to having issues with Catholicism. But these patches of disagreement do not fray his overall connection to the church. David is a musician in his early thirties. He is married to a Protestant woman, and he is bothered by the way his church distinguishes between him and his wife.

"Hard lines are drawn around who's in and who's out," he declares. "When Jesus said, 'This is my body, which is given up for you' and 'This is my blood, which is shed for all,' I interpret this literally. Jesus invites everyone to Eucharist despite the fact that none of us deserve it. Our human institutions are much less welcoming."

It is not hard for David to list other policies of the church that are incongruous with his sense of justice. But he remains Catholic despite these conflicts: "I meet many enlightened people in the church whose values are similar to mine. Although the official church position on these issues is antagonistic, I see God's will being done despite rigid policy." He has visited other corners of organized religion as well and found strengths and faults everywhere he goes. In the end, he returns home to Catholicism.

When asked what is best about being Catholic, David does not hesitate to reply: "Catholics acquire a strong sense of history and devotion through the Mass. When I visit churches that use a less-structured form of worship, I miss this the most. Saying the familiar prayers again and again, each utterance calls my attention to different phrases, and I realize how rich Catholic liturgy is."

David views his religious faith primarily as a personal choice for his own life. For Jim, a father of three young girls, remaining faithful to his Catholic heritage involves what is best for the innocent lives dependent on his care. The clergy sex abuse scandals are at the top of the list of things that cause him to struggle in his relationship with the church.

"I have no words to fully describe the pain, the sadness, and the anger I feel toward these perpetrators," he admits. "Yet I find my faith in the Catholic Church shaken more by those who covered up each and every incident. Those involved in the cover-up were probably very sane individuals motivated by the desire to maintain the power and position of the church and perhaps their individual careers within the church. That hurts the most."

Jim's dissatisfaction with certain aspects of church leadership does not threaten his overall commitment, however. As he puts it, "I feel it is important to separate the theology of the Catholic faith from the institution that runs it. Clearly, the human element of the church is flawed. Yet the theology remains intact."

Jim shares with many Catholics the conviction that the catholicity of the church is its hallmark and its most attractive feature: "To be able to travel across the country and stop anywhere, anytime, at any Catholic church, attend Mass, and feel connected with that congregation is remarkable. The consistency of our faith and the ritual of the Mass, I believe, make that connection. Finally, I relish the opportunity to be part of the heritage and tradition of the church. In an era where secular culture and beliefs change daily, it's a real privilege to be part of an institution that has survived for over two thousand years."

Many people who remain active within the church are not there because of the church per se: the pull is the One who is at the center of it all. For Elaine, a laywoman who works full-time as a pastoral associate in a Catholic parish, the person of Jesus is what keeps her close to a church that often seems far from heaven.

When asked what the best thing about being Catholic is, she responds, "I guess the best thing is knowing who and what I am. I am a follower of Jesus Christ, and I am called to have that shape my life."

But why celebrate that identity in this particular context? "I am reminded of Scripture: 'To whom else shall we go?' Yes, this is the faith that fed my ancestors for generations. Through it, God has kept us all alive and connected to one another. It feels like it's in my DNA. But it's more than just an inheritance for me. I love the image of God-in-Jesus and of life that I find in my church."

One might assume that Elaine has had an easy relationship with the church, considering that she has chosen to make it her life's work. But when asked if she struggles, she sighs and says: "Let me count the ways: The unchristian use of authority and power in the structure of the church bothers me. Our tradition sometimes traps us instead of giving life to us, as with women's limited role in the church, the limited promotion of lay leadership, the unhealthy 'good old boy' network of clergy that protects itself instead of empowering others and the truth. These institutional structures are so often historically based, not theologically grounded."

Far from being deterred or alienated by the conflicts she experiences in the present-day church, she finds her purpose in it all: "My faith makes my life . . . more meaningful." She smiles, adding, "The church also gives me a community of like-minded people to share the journey with. Those people are the closest thing to family I could have."

For Elaine, Jesus makes the ideal of the church worth fighting for. For Tom, a man in his fifties, Jesus is also at the core of his work and his heart.

"There is so much richness and depth to the faith that it takes a decision to be a disciple in order to 'get it,'" Tom says. "We have to take on a whole new way of seeing in order to 'put on Christ,' as St. Paul says. We have to enter into mysteries and paradoxes, one of which is turning to an all-too-fallible institution to access the authentic truths about all creation and our Creator."

Tom can go from expressing the sublime significance of his faith to noting the somewhat ridiculous particulars of it without missing a beat. He recounts an especially bad recent experience with a visiting preacher at his church who went on and on "in a scolding tone, beyond thirty minutes," during Mass. "It seemed arrogant, insensitive, and torturous," Tom says. "Other parts of the Mass were mediocre at best. And then at communion we sang, 'I myself am the bread of life. You and I are the bread of life.' And I was moved to a combination of repentance for my own arrogance and frustration and relief at my true identity—a member of the Body of Christ.

"I don't get that message anywhere else. I hear that I'm a consumer, that I deserve a break today, that I will only be happy with more, more, more, or that we need to bomb and attack other people to be secure. But I don't hear that I am the

Body of Christ, broken and blessed, poured out and shared. And, quite frankly, I need to hear that regularly, because I'm a slow learner and a fast forgetter. That's why I need the church."

What becomes clear after talking with involved and devout Catholics of every age group, political persuasion, and personal style is that the ideal of the "happy Catholic" out there dwelling in blissful contentment with every aspect of his or her life in the church is misleading. A surprising percentage of the folks sitting in the pews (or even in the sanctuary) have been away from the church at some point in their lives. Others have arrived punctually every Sunday, but not without some serious considerations and caveats. Some Catholics have broken the rules and found themselves at great odds with the teachings of the church. Finally, many of the staunchest Catholic adherents have had concerns and bad experiences within their life in the church.

But none of these things move them to sign off altogether and stay home or find a religious path elsewhere. For many, perhaps most, Catholics in the pews, finding a practical peace with the humanity of the church for the sake of its divine elements is a balance worth achieving. This often means making peace with our own humanity as well and accepting the reality that, like St. Paul, we aren't always the Christians we mean to be.

Being a faithful and loyal Catholic, in other words, is not incompatible with the idea of wrestling with and finding instances of dissent in matters that are not essential to the faith. If you have doubts about what the essential faith of the church is, get a copy of the Nicene Creed, the "profession of faith" we make at Mass, and read it carefully and prayerfully. It was written to capture the church's understanding of itself and of the revelation of God, Jesus, and the Holy Spirit. It

is the gold standard of Catholic Christian belief. The rest of
church tradition and teaching is built on this foundation.

If we struggle with other aspects of church policy and
practice, these concerns do not separate us from the faith
of Jesus Christ. Since the informed conscience is the highest
authority to which we must answer, any matter of dissent is a
call for further study, reflection, and prayer on the issues that
give rise to the conflict.

To such prayerful consideration belongs the future of
the church, because every renewal and reform began with a
movement in the hearts of the faithful. The fruits of this labor
of love will sometimes be greater clarity and respect for the
church's position and will on other occasions be an expansion
or reconsidering of the teaching itself. But above all, together
as the church we will achieve the wisdom and understanding
the Holy Spirit promises.

While there are hundreds of reasons to refrain from
receiving the Eucharist, there is only one reason to receive
it: Jesus has invited us to be there and to share in his life. The
centrality of this act makes all other factors regarding church
organization pale in comparison.

Our unity around this table becomes the window through
which we see ourselves as children of God, sisters and
brothers in Christ, and bearers of the Holy Spirit. Nourished
by this meal, we move outward to share the gospel in works
of love, justice, peace, charity, faithfulness, forgiveness, and
hope. It would be a loss to us and the world if we allowed
any secondary matter to keep us from our place at the table,
which is our right according to our baptism, and our greatest
gift from Jesus.

This doesn't mean the pain or the disharmony we may feel
with specific teachings of the church or particular representatives of the institution will just go away. It does mean we have
to decide what we will assign more power to: the pain of the

past or the present call of the Lord. St. Paul reminds us in the letter to the Romans that "neither death, nor life, nor angels, nor rulers, nor things present, nor things to come, nor powers, nor height, nor depth, nor anything else in all creation, will be able to separate us from the love of God in Christ Jesus our Lord." Either Paul is guilty of hyperbole here, or we can be reassured that all the things that seem insurmountable between us and our unity in Christ are more negotiable than we thought.

Robert Frost wrote in his stirring poem "The Death of the Hired Man": "Home is the place where, when you have to go there, / They have to take you in." Members of a family, no matter how fractious their relationships may be, belong to one another in irrevocable ways. In that sense, all baptized Catholics can think of the church as the place where we cannot be denied entrance, no matter "what we've done or failed to do," as we pray at the beginning of Mass. This implies that the door of the church is one that can never be closed and bolted against us. If we want to be there, our right to belong is guaranteed.

It would be dishonest for anyone to promise that a future relationship with the church will be free from the strife involved in the old one. When a separated couple comes back together for a second try, what caused hardship between the couple in the past is bound to be a factor in the future.

But what may have changed is the couple's willingness to talk about the trouble, and they may have a renewed commitment to work things through. Finding a community that is not afraid of honest dialogue will go far toward making sure that past issues do not remain submerged like land mines in the future. Without that dialogue, we are all the poorer. Engaged in that conversation, we ensure that none of the gifts of the Body of Christ will be lost, to the church or to one another.

Archaeology

Charles Wright

from *Poetry*

The older we get, the deeper we dig into our childhoods,
Hoping to find the radiant cell
That washed us, and caused our lives
    to glow in the dark like clock hands
Endlessly turning toward the future,
Tomorrow, day after tomorrow, the day after that,
    all golden, all in good time.

Hiwassee Dam, North Carolina.
    Still 1942,
Still campfire smoke in both our eyes, my brother and I
Gaze far out at the lake in sunflame,
Expecting our father at any moment, like Charon, to appear
Back out of the light from the other side,
    low-gunwaled and loaded down with our slippery
        dreams.

Other incidents flicker like foxfire in the black
Isolate distance of memory,

cross-eyed, horizon-haired.
Which one, is it one, is it any one that cleans us, clears us,
That relimbs our lives to a shining?

One month without rain, two months,
    third month of the new year,
Afternoon breeze-rustle dry in the dry needles of hemlock
        and pine.
I can't get down deep enough.
Sunlight flaps its enormous wings and lifts off from the back
        yard,
The wind rattles its raw throat,
    but I still can't go deep enough.

My Argument with Mario Cuomo

Kenneth L. Woodward

from *Commonweal*

Listening to Democratic presidential nominee John Kerry talk about his position on abortion ("We believe that what matters most is . . . not narrow appeals that divide us, but shared values that unite us . . . "), I hear loudly in the background the sonorous voice of Mario Cuomo, our foremost "philosopher-politician," as the *Boston Globe* crowned him. It is twenty years since Cuomo delivered his famous speech at the University of Notre Dame, in which he defined what has become the established rationale for pro-choice Catholic politicians. I have, in the *New York Times,* dismissed that speech as a piece of "ancient sophistry," a remark that brought a message from the former governor of New York urging me to reexamine his words. And so I have. I have also tracked Cuomo's statements on the abortion issue in this political season and discussed the matter with him by phone.

A whole new generation, including Senator Kerry, has come of political age since 1984, when Cuomo's speech was seen as a defense not only of his own pro-choice politics but also those of Geraldine Ferraro, a Catholic congresswoman from New York who was that year's Democratic candidate for vice president of the United States. Since then, Cuomo's apologia has been enshrined in books by and about him, highlighted in recent histories of American Catholicism by John T. McGreevy and Peter Steinfels, and echoed by the forty-eight members of Congress who recently asserted that "as Catholics we do not believe it is our role to legislate the teachings of the Catholic Church." It is, then, a kind of benchmark statement that is worth revisiting to see what his arguments were and whether they hold up.

Mario Cuomo, it should be recalled, served three terms as governor of New York. In 1984 there was talk of his running for president eventually, which later he nearly did. In the month or so before his Notre Dame speech he was the subject of a flattering cover story in *Newsweek*. He had already been invited to Notre Dame to speak on the relationship between religion and politics when he happened to catch a Sunday morning interview with then-archbishop John J. O'Connor on television. Under questioning, O'Connor said he could not see how a Catholic in good conscience could support abortion rights. When asked if excommunication should be leveled against any Catholic politician who did, O'Connor said he'd have to think that over. A thicker-skinned politician might have let the comment pass, especially one so casually made. But Cuomo took it as a personal challenge, and at Notre Dame he would respond.

In his speech at Notre Dame, the governor declared that as a Catholic and as a matter of conscience, he regarded abortion as "sinful." But this, he insisted, was his "private" view as an "obedient" Catholic raised in the "pre–Vatican II" church. As a politician and public official, however, Cuomo said, he was not obliged to work for laws that reflected Catholic "dogmas," citing among other examples the fact that the bishops themselves no longer sought through laws to oblige non-Catholics to observe church teachings on birth control. While acknowledging that abortion is a graver moral issue than contraception, Cuomo further argued that it would be both wrong and impractical to seek laws restricting abortion. He gave two reasons. First, such laws would oblige non-Catholics and Catholics who disagree with the church's teachings on abortion, thereby violating their religious freedom: "We know that the price of seeking to force our beliefs on others is that they might someday force theirs on us." Second, since there is no public consensus in support of antiabortion legislation, any efforts to pass such laws would be divisive and unenforceable: "The values derived from religious belief will not—and should not—be accepted as part of the public morality unless they are shared by the pluralistic community at large, by consensus."

At this point it is worth noting what Cuomo did not say, as well as what he did.

Never once did he say that abortion was evil, intrinsically or otherwise.

Never once did he say—as the bishops had, as he himself could have—that opposition to abortion as a matter of public morality was a defense of the human rights of the unborn.

Never once did he say that the abortion dispute was a disagreement over the scope of social justice.

He did not say these things, and never has, I believe, because doing so would make his position difficult if not impossible to defend.

He did not say these things, and never has, because, as I think his record makes clear, he does not believe them to be true.

In his book *A People Adrift,* Peter Steinfels cautions against twisting Cuomo's argument "into the crude formula, 'I am personally opposed to abortion but I don't want to impose my view on others.'" In fact, Cuomo's argument strikes me as even cruder than that. It says that his reasons for thinking abortion "sinful" are not only "private" but sectarian as well. Thus, while formally rejecting the notion that Catholic opposition to abortion on demand (another phrase he avoids) violates separation of church and state, Cuomo advances a rationale (the church has told him so) that bolsters the case for advancing just such a charge. It was, withal, a carefully crafted speech. Cuomo sought to defend both his docility toward church teachings and his right—indeed, his duty—to act against them.

In a public dialogue on religion and American politics recently published by the Brookings Institution (*One Electorate under God?*), Cuomo repeats the arguments he made at Notre Dame (applying them to church teachings on stem-cell research as well) in order to defend his continuing support for unrestricted abortion rights. But as Robert George, a professor of jurisprudence at Princeton, points out in a devastating rebuttal, the fact that any religious body opposes the killing of the unborn—or owning slaves, or exploiting workers—does not mean that laws protecting the unborn, outlawing slavery, or requiring that workers be paid a just wage violate the freedom of religion of those who do not accept those teachings.

But what are we to make of Cuomo's argument, first elaborated at Notre Dame, that there is no public "consensus" regarding abortion?

I take it he meant, and still means, that there is no political majority to support any restrictions on public access to abortion, not to mention recriminalization. Politically, he may be right. But how would Cuomo know, since he has never mustered the political courage to test his own assumptions?

In fact, there has long been a moral consensus regarding abortion that, if anything, now tilts toward the pro-life position. Indeed, if there were no such current running counter to *Roe v. Wade,* abortion would no longer be a political issue. Even at the time of Cuomo's Notre Dame speech, polls showed that while most Americans supported the right to abortion, pluralities of various sizes believed that abortion should be restricted to the rare and so-called hard cases of rape, incest, and immediate physical harm to the mother. A 1987 study of why women have abortions, conducted by the pro-choice Alan Guttmacher Institute, showed that most women chose abortion for a mix of three reasons: giving birth would interfere with work, school, or other responsibilities; lack of financial support; and lack of a relationship—or "relationship problems" —with the father usually. By the mid-1990s, the number of women identifying themselves as pro-life began to match the number identifying as pro-choice. Last year, a poll sponsored by another pro-choice organization found that 51 percent of women wanted abortion either not permitted or restricted to the hard cases. This April, a Zogby poll found that 56 percent of all Americans would abolish or severely restrict abortion rights—a figure that reached 60.5 percent among those eighteen to twenty-nine years of age.

Given his celebrated intellect and powers of persuasion, Cuomo might have nurtured this emerging moral consensus into political expression. In his Notre Dame speech he conceded as much: "And surely, I can, if so inclined, demand some kind of law against abortion not because my bishops say it is wrong but because I think that the whole community, regardless of its religious beliefs, should agree on the importance of protecting life—including life in the womb, which is at the very least potentially human and should not be extinguished casually."

This teasing way of letting his listeners know that he was aware that this argument and option were open to him was, in fact, Cuomo's way of telling them that the option was merely private—a "prudential" judgment that no one could make for him. But his words led not a few in his audience to assume that he would use his influence to modify his party's embrace of abortion on demand, should the opportunity arise. God knows, he had his chances.

In 1988, the Democrats dropped from their platform a mild statement recognizing "the religious and ethical concerns which many Americans have about abortion." Cuomo said not a word of objection. At the 1992 convention in New York City, where the Clinton forces proclaimed the Democrats the party of the "big tent," Cuomo again stood by as the Clintonites silenced the pro-life Catholic governor of Pennsylvania, Robert P. Casey. Casey, who was at least as liberal as Cuomo and far more effective as a governor, had asked to read a minority report challenging the platform's endorsement of abortion as a "fundamental right" deserving of government funding. Instead, in introducing Clinton to the convention, Cuomo twice denounced Republican opposition to abortion. I was standing just behind Governor Casey's empty seat when Cuomo brought the delegates to their feet in extended applause with this line: "We need a leader who will stop the Republican attempt, through laws and through the courts, to tell us what god to believe in and how to apply that god's judgment to our schoolrooms, our bedrooms, and our bodies." Stripped of the overheated partisan rhetoric, is this god he so derides not the same god who privately instructs Cuomo the Catholic that abortion is "sinful"? Here we see the whole intent of Cuomo's Notre Dame speech—the spurious justification of a Catholic politician who wants it both ways.

When I spoke by phone with Cuomo in June, I asked him why he did not deploy the same passion on behalf of abortion that he used in fighting the consensus—even in New York State—supporting capital punishment.

"The argument I made against capital punishment," he said in quick reply, "was not a moral argument." But the truth is that Cuomo never gave a speech that did not glisten with the sweat of moral conviction, and his campaign against capital punishment was no exception. In *One Electorate under God?* he explains his opposition to state-sanctioned capital punishment: "I am against the death penalty because I think it is bad and unfair. It is debasing. It is degenerate. It kills innocent people." That is exactly the kind of moral argument pro-life people make against abortion and its funding by government.

Neither logic nor consistency has been the hallmark of our foremost "philosopher-politician." He has convinced himself, it seems to me, that "moral" arguments can proceed only from what he calls religious "dogmas," and thus cannot be used in making arguments in the public square. And this is precisely the kind of reasoning that sustains the pro-choice position of our most prominent current Catholic politician, John Kerry.

In my conversation with Cuomo, he impressed on me the need for a church-wide Catholic discussion of "When does life begin?" According to biographer David Maraniss, Bill Clinton once put the same question to a Baptist pastor, who cited Genesis in assuring him that life begins—as it did for Adam—at the first drawing of breath. But Catholics are not biblical fundamentalists who can anchor abortion rights with a biblical story. *That* would indeed be arguing abortion from a purely religious perspective. The Catholic argument is broader, advancing philosophical, political, and even biological warrants. I reminded Cuomo that a human embryo can never turn out to be a cat or dog, which is why the church-wide discussion he wants would quickly prove moot.

After reviewing Cuomo on the subject of abortion, it is clear to me where he stands. He is not sure that a developing fetus—never mind an embryo—is really human. The human "family" that he so often summons up in his political rhetoric is not wide enough to include the unborn. Catholics have every reason to repudiate the argument he has bequeathed to pro-choice politicians of both parties.

The Cross and the Empty Tomb

The Editors of *America*

from *America*

In Bach's oratorio *The Saint John Passion,* a bass aria begins:
Eilt . . . (Hurry, hurry, you suffering souls . . .)
And in an urgent whisper, the chorus responds:
Wohin . . . (Where to?)
And the soloist replies:
Nach Golgotha . . . (To Calvary . . .)
That chorus represents the whole human family in two ways. On the one hand, Christian faith teaches that by his cross Jesus redeemed all men and women. On the other hand, history and experience teach that for the most part, the face of humanity is stained with blood and tears.

Even those whose existence is comfortable must sooner or later confront death. Even in the United States in 2004, there are millions for whom misery is the daily climate—the poor, the homeless, the jobless, the bereaved, and those who are seriously ill.

"If it weren't for hard luck," said a Texas sharecropper once, "I wouldn't have no luck at all."

For nearly two thousand years, however, believers have found that the mystery of the cross can comfort and strengthen hearts pressed down by sorrow. In every century, saints have given their fellow Christians the same advice the Bach libretto gives. St. Paul told the Romans they would be glorified with Christ, provided they suffered with him. St. Thomas More reminded his children in times of trouble that they could hardly hope to go to heaven on a feather bed, seeing that our Lord went there on a cross.

In the twentieth century, Edith Stein, who was canonized in 1998, was a preeminent witness to the cross. She was born into a German Jewish family in 1891 and was baptized in 1922. In 1933 she entered the Carmelite convent in Cologne, Germany, where she was given the name Teresa Benedicta of the Cross.

That name was prophetic. In a lecture she gave in 1931, Edith Stein said: "Whoever belongs to Christ must go the whole way with him. He must mature to adulthood: he must one day or other walk the way of the cross to Gethsemane and Golgotha." She herself walked that way in August 1942, when she was put to death in the gas chambers of Auschwitz.

All the same, Edith Stein, who had a gift for sympathizing with others, would surely have agreed that Christians must be wary of too easy comment on the mystery of the cross. There is good reason for this diffidence. Suffering is too common to be interesting, too terrible to be taken for granted, and too mysterious to be understood by the human mind left to itself.

Let one example underscore that point. In December 1966, Pierre Veuillot, then fifty-three, became archbishop of Paris and was promptly made a cardinal. Within a few months, he was stricken with cancer, and he died in February 1968.

During the last weeks of his life, in great pain, he said to a visitor: "Tell priests not to speak of suffering. They don't know what they're talking about. They don't know what it is."

All the same, if Christians must be circumspect in recommending consideration of the cross to others, they must be ready to recommend such meditation to themselves. When they do so, they will catch a glimpse of the meaning that suffering can have when it is looked at in the light of the death and resurrection of the Lord.

In the prayer he made in Gethsemane, Jesus asked his Father to spare him the agonizing death he foresaw. But then he added at once the words that have ever since supported countless Christians in their own sufferings: "Not my will, but thine be done." Under the impulse of the love that he bore for his eternal Father and his earthly brothers and sisters, Christ chose to walk the way of the cross in fulfillment of his mission to make salvation available to all men and women. The cross was a vehicle of love: "Ours were the sufferings he bore."

This revelation of the meaning that suffering can have provides an austere comfort. It does not anesthetize pain. It does not unveil the final and complete answer to the problem of evil, but it promises those who believe that there will be such an answer at the end of time, because the death of Jesus was followed by his resurrection.

Christians are precisely the people who believe not just that Jesus died but that he rose on the third day and lives in glory. In a note to her prioress a few months before her death, Edith Stein wrote that she could say from the heart, "*Ave crux, spes unica*"—"Hail cross, our only hope." But if Calvary had not been followed by the Resurrection, there would be no such hope. If Christ is not risen from the dead, said Paul to the Corinthians, then our faith is vain.

But he has risen, and so death, the last enemy, has been destroyed. Christians are a people of hope because they believe that the story of the human family will have a happy ending. The joy of Easter is imperishable, because on the first Easter morning the tomb in the garden was empty.

Contributors

America is a Catholic weekly magazine that was founded in 1909 by the Jesuits of the United States.

Mark Bosco, SJ, is an assistant professor of both English and theology at Loyola University Chicago and the author of *Graham Greene's Catholic Imagination.*

Alice L. Camille is a writer and religious educator. She is the author of *Invitation to the New Testament: A Catholic Approach to the Christian Scriptures* and, with Joel Schorn, *A Faith Interrupted: An Honest Conversation with Alienated Catholics.*

The late **Dorothy Day** was a bluntly eloquent American saint who matters enormously to those of us chasing after mercy in this violent world—which is to say, all of us. Among her other feats, she was the cofounder of the Catholic Worker movement; for more on that riveting idea, see www.catholicworker.org. Her books include *The Long Loneliness,* an autobiography first published in 1952.

Rod Dreher is an editorial writer and a columnist for the *Dallas Morning News.*

David James Duncan is the author of two popular novels, *The River Why* and *The Brothers K,* and two collections of essays and stories, *River Teeth* and *My Story As Told by Water,* the latter of which was a finalist for the National Book Award. His work appears regularly in *Orion* magazine, for which he and Wendell Berry cowrote the book *Citizens Dissent: Security, Morality, and Leadership in an Age of Terror.*

Paul Elie, a senior editor at Farrar, Straus and Giroux, is the author of *The Life You Save May Be Your Own: An American Pilgrimage.* He has been a contributor to *Commonweal,* the *New York Times Magazine,* the *New Republic,* and other magazines.

Gregory D. Foster is a professor of political science at the Industrial College of the Armed Forces, National Defense University, Washington, D.C. A West Point graduate, he was an infantry company commander with the American Division during the Vietnam War. He is the author of *In Search of a Post-Cold War Security Structure,* among other books.

Ron Hansen is the Gerard Manley Hopkins, SJ, Professor in the Arts and Humanities at Santa Clara University. He is the author of many novels, most notably *Mariette in Ecstasy, Atticus,* and *Hitler's Niece.* His most recent work is *Isn't It Romantic?*

Austen Ivereigh is deputy editor of the *Tablet,* the international Catholic weekly newspaper based in London. He edited *Unfinished Journey: The Church Forty Years after Vatican II.*

Michael Mack is an associate professor of English at The Catholic University of America. He is the author of *Sidney's Poetics: Imitating Creation* and is currently working on a book about the mysterious genius William Shakespeare.

Paul Mariani is a professor of literature and writing at Boston College and the author of many books of poetry, essays, and biography. Among the lives he has limned are those of William Carlos Williams, Hart Crane, and John Berryman. He is also the author of the spiritual adventure *Thirty Days: On Retreat with the Exercises of St. Ignatius.*

James Martin, SJ, is an associate editor of *America* magazine. His books include *In Good Company: The Fast Track from the Corporate World to Poverty, Chastity, and Obedience,* an account of his curious road to the priesthood. He often writes the column "Of Many Things" in *America.*

Sophie Masson is a writer who lives in New South Wales, Australia. Born in Jakarta, Indonesia, and raised in Australia and France, she is an essayist and the author of many young adult and children's books. Her more than twenty novels include *The Hoax.*

Thomas A. Nelson is retired after many years with the Ford Motor Company. He lives in Farmington Hills, Michigan.

Barbara Nicolosi is a screenwriter and the executive director of Act One, Inc., a nonprofit organization devoted to the training and formation of writers and executives who are Christians. Her articles have appeared in a number of Catholic publications, and her blog, Church of the Masses (http://www.churchofthemasses.blogspot.com), is entertaining, insightful, and opinionated, especially about films.

Cynthia Ozick is the author of many books of fiction and essays, most recently the novel *Heir to the Glimmering World.* Readers curious about Ozick should read her novels *The Shawl* and *The Messiah of Stockholm,* or any of her essay collections. An excellent introduction to her work is *A Cynthia Ozick Reader,* published by Indiana University Press.

Pattiann Rogers is a prize-winning poet and essayist whose ten books of poems include *Firekeeper, Song of the World Becoming,* and, most recently, *Generations.*

James V. Schall, SJ, is a professor of political theory at Georgetown University and the áuthor of many books, including *Schall on Chesterton: Timely Essays on Timeless Paradoxes.* His articles are widely published, and he is also a columnist for *Crisis* and *Gilbert Magazine.*

Joel Schorn has worked as an editor for several Catholic publications. He is the coauthor, with Alice L. Camille, of *A Faith Interrupted: An Honest Conversation with Alienated Catholics.*

David Scott is the author of *A Revolution of Love: The Meaning of Mother Teresa,* from which the essay that appears in this anthology was gently extracted. He is the editorial director of the St. Paul Center for Biblical Theology in Pittsburgh, where he edits the academic journal *Letter & Spirit.* His books include *The Catholic Passion: Rediscovering the Power and Beauty of the Faith* and *Weapons of the Spirit: Selected Writings of Father John Hugo* (with Mike Aquilina).

Monsignor Robert Sokolowski is the Elizabeth Breckenridge Caldwell Professor of Philosophy at The Catholic University of America. His many books include *Eucharistic Presence: A Study in the Theology of Disclosure.*

Kevin M. Tortorelli is a Franciscan priest at St. Francis of Assisi Church in New York City.

August Turak, founder of the Self Knowledge Symposium Foundation (SKSF), won the first Power of Purpose Award from the John Templeton Foundation for the essay reprinted

in this anthology. The Self Knowledge Symposium (www.
selfknowledge.org) is an interfaith nonprofit group devoted
to helping people find a deeper and more spiritual purpose
to their lives; the Templeton Foundation (www.templeton.
org) supports "programs, competitions, publications, and
studies in the human sciences and in character education that
promote the exploration of the spiritual nature of the human
person." For information on the Power of Purpose Awards,
see www.powerofpurpose.org.

George Weigel is a senior fellow and director of the
Catholic Studies program at the Ethics and Public Policy
Center. He is the author of *Witness to Hope: The Biography
of Pope John Paul II* and *The Cube and the Cathedral: Europe,
America, and Politics without God.*

Kenneth L. Woodward, a contributing editor at *Newsweek,*
was the religion editor at that magazine for nearly forty
years. He is the author of *Making Saints* and, most recently,
The Book of Miracles.

Charles Wright is an award-winning poet and an essayist.
His many books of poetry include *Country Music,* which won
the National Book Award; the Pulitzer prize-winning *Black
Zodiac;* and the recent *Buffalo Yoga.* He is the Souder Family
Professor of English at the University of Virginia.

Emily Wu is a writer who lives in Cupertino, California.
Her work has appeared in the *San Jose Mercury News, Xingdao
Daily,* the Chinese edition of *Reader's Digest,* and many other
journals in English and Chinese. She is at work on an autobiography titled *Feathers in the Storm.*

Don Wycliff is the public editor of the *Chicago Tribune*, a position he has held since 2000. He was previously the *Tribune*'s editorial page director, and he has served as a reporter or an editor for the *New York Times*, the *Chicago Sun-Times*, and the *Chicago Daily News*.

Acknowledgments

From Brian Doyle, editor, *The Best Catholic Writing 2005*

Loyola Press's Best Catholic Writing is an annual collection, and all manner of written work concerning Catholic life is eligible for inclusion in the next volume, *The Best Catholic Writing 2006*. I will consider all writing that is true, remarkable, and Catholic-minded in the largest possible sense.

Please send me any articles, essays, poems, short stories, plays, speeches, sermons, elegies, eulogies, monologues, rants, raves, etc., that have been written or published in 2004 or 2005. I will also consider book excerpts and yet-to-be-published writings.

Send nominated entries to me by fax, e-mail attachment, or snail mail at

Brian Doyle
Portland Magazine
University of Portland
5000 N. Willamette Boulevard
Portland, OR 97203
bdoyle@up.edu
503 943 7202 phone
503 943 7178 fax

A Special Invitation
from Loyola Press

Loyola Press invites you to become one of our Loyola Press Advisors! Join our unique online community of people willing to share with us their thoughts and ideas about Catholic life and faith. By sharing your perspective, you will help us improve our books and serve the greater Catholic community.

From time to time, registered advisors are invited to participate in online surveys and discussion groups. Most surveys will take less than ten minutes to complete. Loyola Press will recognize your time and efforts with gift certificates and prizes. Your personal information will be held in strict confidence. Your participation will be for research purposes only, and at no time will we try to sell you anything.

Please consider this opportunity to help Loyola Press improve our products and better serve you and the Catholic community. To learn more or to join, visit **www.SpiritedTalk.org** and register today.